WAKEHURST PLACE, in the beautiful High Weald of Sussex, is an outstanding botanic garden and conservation area, managed by the Royal Botanic Gardens, Kew. Wakehurst Place has a mild, friendly climate, a high rainfall and moisture-retentive soils, complementing the conditions at Kew and allowing many important groups of plants, unable to be grown successfully at Kew, to flourish here. Above all, Wakehurst Place, which is leased from the National Trust, offers what is unavailable at Kew - room to expand.

This booklet is both a practical guide to the gardens and woodland walks, the specimens and conservation efforts; and a souvenir, with more detailed information about the history, purpose and future of Wakehurst Place, Kew Gardens and the most recent addition, the Millennium Seed Bank.

Wakehurst Place is a respected botanic garden of international importance. Under the stewardship of the Royal Botanic Gardens, Kew, it has become a living green museum, mixing botanical science with horticulture, highlighting the importance of plant conservation for the future of viable life on earth.

The estate's journey to the present day has been long. People have lived in these Wealden woodlands and valleys since at least the Iron Age. A Roman road once ran past Wakehurst, the name itself is Saxon, and the first recorded owner was a Norman who arrived with William the Conqueror.

The present mansion, in Ardingly sandstone with a Horsham-tiled roof, was built in 1590 by Sir Edward Culpeper - a distant relative of Nicholas, the famous herbalist - and retains its imposing Tudor facade. However, the last of the Culpepers sold the estate to pay off gambling debts in 1694, when it was bought by Dennis Lydell, an eventual Royal Navy associate of Samuel Pepys, who enlarged the estate to 3,100 acres in 1748.

Gerald Loder

2

brief history

The Peytons, another significant family, were resident from 1776 to 1869, when it was sold to the Dowager Marchioness of Downshire, who probably started planting some of the large exotic trees, such as the giant redwoods, during her time here.

After Sir William Boord, who owned the estate from 1890 to 1902, it was Gerald Loder, later Lord Wakehurst, who started to develop the gardens with enormous enthusiasm and great skill. He was a passionate plantsman and helped sponsor many collecting expeditions at the turn of the century, particularly to eastern Asia, still acknowledged to be the world's richest source of temperate flora. He was keenly interested in Southern Hemisphere plants and built up an outstanding collection from South America, Australia and New Zealand.

On Loder's death, Wakehurst Place was bought by Sir Henry Price who was equally passionate about plants and in his care the estate matured wonderfully richly and became widely admired. In 1963, Sir Henry bequeathed Wakehurst Place, with a sizeable endowment, to the National Trust from whom it was leased, on 1st January 1965, for the benefit of the Royal Botanic Gardens, Kew.

Sir Henry Price

Note: There are more details on the Mansion and its history, together with the story of successive collections and plantings, later on in this book, on pp 78-89.

Wakehurst Place:

Few visitors to Wakehurst Place have an accurate idea of the size and scope of the estate. The Mansion, together with the more formal gardens nearby; the woodland walks and now, the Millennium Seed Bank, are normally the furthest extent of most visitors' mental picture of Wakehurst Place.

Those who have been to the Loder Valley Nature Reserve know there is more to Wakehurst than meets the eye, but even they may be surprised by this overall plan of the estate, shown here for the first time in this form.

The estate at Wakehurst Place extends to around 188 hectares (465 acres). It can be divided roughly into three: the gardens and woodland walks, 73 ha (180 acres); Loder Valley Nature Reserve, 60 ha (149 acres); while the outlying parkland and woodland cover 55 ha (136 acres).

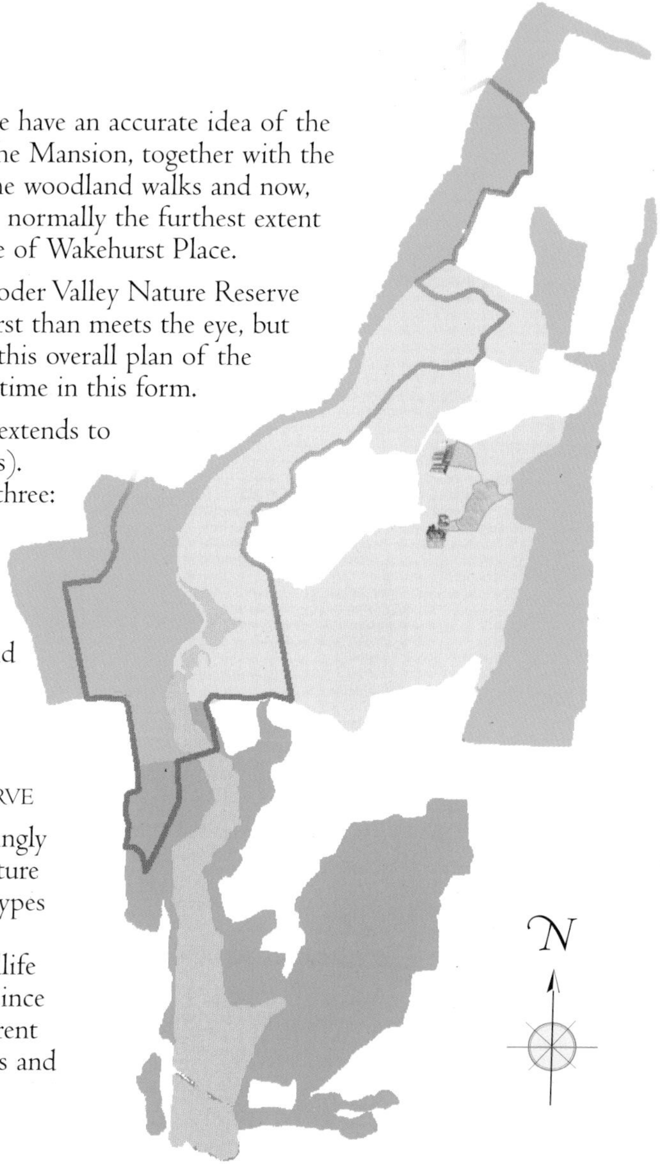

LODER VALLEY NATURE RESERVE

Incorporating a branch of Ardingly Reservoir, the Loder Valley Nature Reserve embraces three major types of local habitat; woodland, meadowland and wetland. Wildlife conservation follows naturally since each habitat is suited to a different range of plants, birds, mammals and invertebrates (see pp 66-67).

SITE OF SPECIAL SCIENTIFIC INTEREST (SSSI)

The Wakehurst and Chiddingly Woods SSSI was designated for its valuable communities of ferns, mosses, liverworts and lichens growing on the sandstone outcrops (also see pp 52 & 73). Its extent on the estate is shown here by the grey line .

MANSION GARDENS & WOODLAND WALKS

The gardens around the Mansion are where most of the ornamental plants are and are also the easiest part for wheelchair users. Visitors can easily spend their entire visit here, with a diversion to the Millennium Seed Bank. Woodland walks take visitors through the temperate regions of the world, from Himalayan slopes and Rocky Mountain coastline, to traditional British woodlands.

OUTLYING PARKLAND AND WOODLAND

English Heritage classify Wakehurst Place as a Grade 2 historic house and parkland and the estate is managed to conserve it as such. Forestry work undertaken in the outlying woodland includes the development of conifer species as commercial Christmas trees and hardwood coppicing for charcoal production (see pp 74-75).

N

the greater estate

Follow any pathway to the west of the Mansion and your walk takes you via the Southern Hemisphere Garden, through the Pinetum to the Himalayan Glade and on to Westwood Lake. There you can choose to return by Westwood Valley and the Water Gardens; or continue through Horsebridge Wood, the Rock Walk, Bethlehem Wood and finally the Millennium Seed Bank. The first walk takes approximately one hour, the second about one and a half hours.

A gentle stroll around the complete circumference of Wakehurst - some 3.6 km (2.3 miles) - takes around two hours.

Follow the pathway to the north of the Millennium Seed Bank and your walk takes you to Bethlehem Wood and the Birch Trail, the Rock Walk, Coates Wood and Bloomer's Valley.

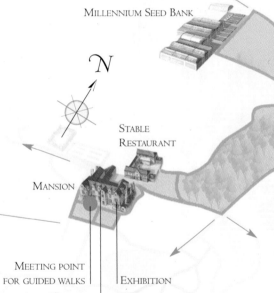

MILLENNIUM SEED BANK

N

STABLE RESTAURANT

MANSION

MEETING POINT FOR GUIDED WALKS

EXHIBITION

GIFT SHOP

KEEP ON THE GRASS!

At Wakehurst, you can walk virtually anywhere you like, except where it doesn't make sense, such as in flower beds. Lawns, grass paths, they're there to be used. Try to take the more scenic route - it's usually very rewarding.

CAR PARK

Pathways to the south or east of the Mansion lead to the Mansion Pond, Tony Schilling Asian Heath Garden, the Slips and Water Garden. Here you may decide to continue through Westwood Valley and further, or return via the Himalayan Glade, Pinetum and the Southern Hemisphere Garden. There are too many options to give accurate timings, but the maps on the following pages give all the information needed to decide on a suitable walk.

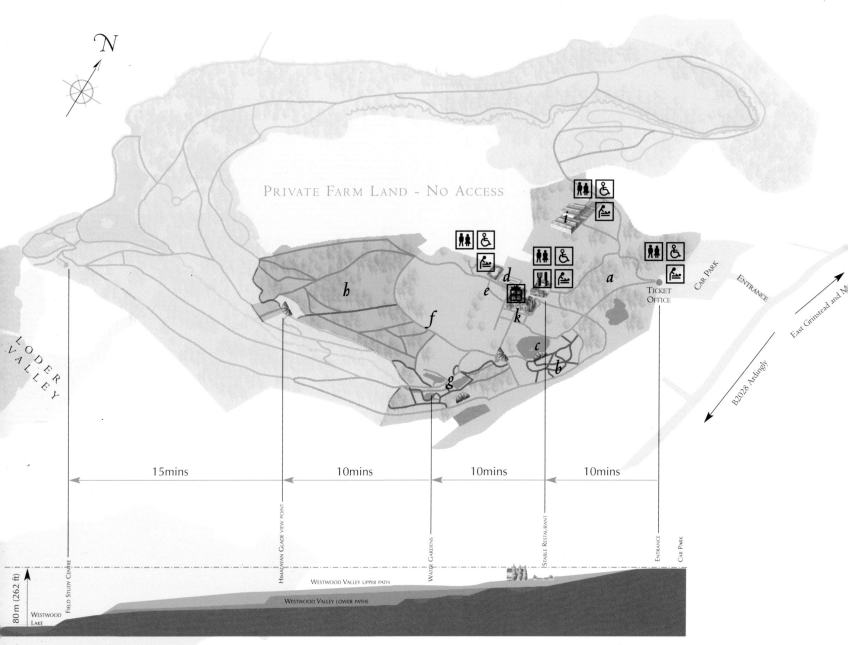

PRIVATE FARM LAND - NO ACCESS

N

LODER VALLEY

h

f

e

d

k

g

c

b

a

i

TICKET OFFICE

CAR PARK

ENTRANCE

East Grinstead and M

B2028 Ardingly

15mins

10mins

10mins

10mins

WESTWOOD LAKE

FIELD STUDY CENTRE

HIMALAYAN GLADE VIEW POINT

WATER GARDENS

STABLE RESTAURANT

ENTRANCE

CAR PARK

80 m (262 ft)

WESTWOOD VALLEY upper path

WESTWOOD VALLEY lower paths

6

What to see:- Mansion and Gardens, Millennium Seed Bank

BELOW ARE BRIEF DETAILS OF PLACES YOU MIGHT LIKE TO SEE NEAR THE MANSION. THEY ARE KEYED TO THE MAP OPPOSITE, WHICH SHOWS HOW TO GET THERE. FOR MORE DETAILS, TURN TO THE PAGE NUMBER GIVEN. PLEASE TAKE CARE ON THE STEEPER PATHS AND REMEMBER IT MAY BE WET UNDERFOOT EVEN ON DRY DAYS. MOST AREAS HERE ARE SUITABLE FOR WHEELCHAIR ACCESS - TO HELP, DIFFERENT TYPES OF PATH ARE SHOWN IN VARIOUS COLOURS ON THE MAP.

ENTRANCE GROUNDS The trees and shrubs here are selected for autumn colour. After entering, fork right for the Millennium Seed Bank, or left to the Mansion and main gardens. In summer, there's a small garden centre on your way out.

TONY SCHILLING ASIAN HEATH GARDEN *p 12.* Here, you'll find ideas for plants in exposed sites, as they come from Asian mountain heights. Mostly dwarf in habit, they include rhododendrons, cotoneasters, potentillas and more.

MANSION POND AND SPRING BORDER *p 24.* Here are fine specimen plants including Japanese maples and rhododendrons, while the rock terrace is carpeted with low-growing perennials.

THE WALLED GARDENS *pp 14-17.* Doubly rewarding:- the Sir Henry Price Garden is a gem of a 'cottage' garden; while The Pleasaunce is a more formal design around a pool and fountain.

THE WINTER GARDEN *p 18.* At its best between December and March, traditional winter interest plants are mixed here with less well known species. Various dogwoods, willows and ornamental grasses are a delight.

SOUTHERN HEMISPHERE GARDEN & SPECIMEN BEDS *pp 20-23.* These contain rare shrubs and trees from South America, Australia and New Zealand. The Specimen Beds show brilliant summer colour and the hypericums and skimmias are National Collections.

THE SLIPS AND WATER GARDENS *pp 26-29.* The Slips leads you down past mature magnolias, pieris and dogwoods. Marginal and aquatic plants display colour from May to October. The intimate Iris Dell with its waterfall is enclosed by Japanese maples and rhododendrons.

THE PINETUM *p 30.* Ravaged by the Great Storm of 1987, the Pinetum has been successfully replanted with conifers from Europe, North America, Asia, and the Southern Hemisphere.

MILLENNIUM SEED BANK *pp 60-65.* The world's largest and most comprehensive conservation project aims to safeguard 24,000 species of plants from around the world and secure the future of all of Britain's native flora. Fascinating interactive displays and videos.

KEY TO MAP

 Toilets

 Stable Restaurant

 Viewpoint and photo opportunity

 Baby changing

Shop

THE MANSION AND HISTORY *pp 78-91.* The story of Wakehurst Place and its dedicated plant collectors, the involvement of the Royal Botanic Gardens, Kew and its activities now and in the future - all the historical background of the estate is here.

 Toilet - Wheelchair access

Shelters and alcoves

STAR FEATURES Wherever there is a plant or garden feature of special interest, it is given a paragraph to itself, marked with a star symbol

Made up paths suitable for wheelchair access

Unmade, gravel or bark paths, steep and uneven in places

Grass paths defined by mowing in summer, less obvious in winter

Steep or slippery paths - take care and keep children under close supervision

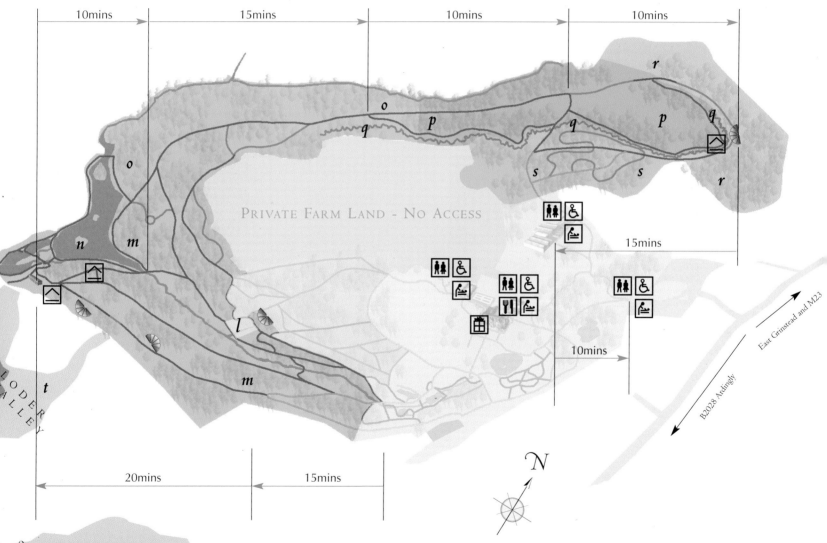

70 m (229 ft)

FIELD STUDY CENTRE

COATES WOOD

HORSEBRIDGE WOOD   UPPER PATH AND ROCK WALK

BLOOMER'S VALLEY

WESTWOOD LAKE

10mins   15mins   10mins   10mins

15mins

r

o

q   *p*   *q*   *p*   *q*

s   *s*   *r*

PRIVATE FARM LAND - NO ACCESS

o

10mins

n   *m*

l

t   *m*

20mins   15mins

LODER
VALLEY

East Grinstead and M23

B2028 Ardingly

N

What to see:-Woodlands, Wetlands, Loder Valley

BELOW ARE BRIEF DETAILS OF PLACES YOU MIGHT LIKE TO SEE IN THE LARGE EXPANSE OF THE GARDENS DEVOTED TO TREE COLLECTIONS AND LOCAL HABITATS. THEY ARE KEYED TO THE MAP OPPOSITE, WHICH SHOWS HOW TO GET THERE. FOR MORE DETAILS, TURN TO THE PAGE NUMBER GIVEN. PLEASE TAKE CARE ON THE STEEPER PATHS AND REMEMBER IT MAY BE WET UNDERFOOT EVEN ON DRY DAYS. THERE ARE FEW PATHS SUITABLE FOR WHEELCHAIR ACCESS HERE - TO HELP, DIFFERENT TYPES OF PATH ARE SHOWN IN VARIOUS COLOURS ON THE MAP.

HIMALAYAN GLADE *p 32*. Were you 3,000 m (9,800 ft) up in the mountains, you would see vegetation like this - secondary woodland of cotoneaster, berberis and birches, rhododendrons and firs.

WESTWOOD VALLEY *pp 36-39*. This recreates the woodlands of eastern Asia, possibly the world's richest temperate habitat for plants with over 4,000 species. Most semi-evergreen favourites are here - and the bluebells in spring.

WESTWOOD LAKE AND WETLANDS *pp 40-43*. Westwood Lake and the Wetland Conservation Area keep valuable Sussex habitats alive for their characteristic plant and animal life.

HORSEBRIDGE WOOD *pp 44-47*. Much of pre-Columbian America was vast primeval forest. In Horsebridge Wood, six of America's seven forest areas are represented from maples of the eastern Appalachians to giant sequoias from the Pacific coast.

BLOOMER'S VALLEY *pp 48-51*. Agricultural land until the 1960s, this sweeping grassland valley is fringed with trees from Europe, the near East and Mediterranean. Other exotics include splendid monkey-puzzle trees from South America.

ROCK WALK *p 52*. These rugged outcrops of Ardingly sandstone in Wakehurst's damp, shady woodlands are a Site of Special Scientific Interest for the mosses, liverworts, lichens and ferns growing on the rocks.

COATES WOOD *pp 54-57*. Step into Southern Hemisphere temperate forest with the National Collection of southern beeches. To date, 17 species have been collected, still young but here, safe to grow.

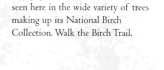
BETHLEHEM WOOD *p 58*. Birches are very popular trees and just why can be seen here in the wide variety of trees making up its National Birch Collection. Walk the Birch Trail.

LODER VALLEY NATURE RESERVE & CONSERVATION *pp 66-77*. This is living conservation and restoration at its best, preserving not only habitats complete with wildlife, but also traditional countryside management.

KEY TO MAP

 Toilets

 Baby changing

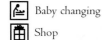 Toilet - Wheelchair access

Stable Restaurant

Shop

Shelters and alcoves

Viewpoint and photo opportunity

✱ STAR FEATURES Wherever there is a plant or garden feature of special interest, it is given a paragraph to itself, marked with a star symbol

Made up paths suitable for wheelchair access

Unmade, gravel or bark paths, steep and uneven in places

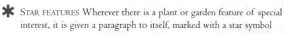
Grass paths defined by mowing in summer, less obvious in winter

Steep or slippery paths - take care and keep children under close supervision

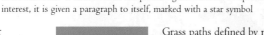

The Gardens, Mansion and Millennium Seed Bank

This section of the Guide is about the gardens near the Mansion at Wakehurst Place. On the following pages, each garden is described in more detail:- the type of garden it is, what plants grow there and when they look their best.

While the house has been here for over 400 years, the gardens started to take their present shape around the turn of the century, being developed from 1903 by Gerald Loder (later Lord Wakehurst) and head gardener Alfred Coates; and then by Sir Henry Price.

A major attraction at Wakehurst Place is the range of rarely seen plants from South America and Australasia. There are also four National Collections within the grounds - birches, southern beeches, skimmias and hypericums or St. John's worts.

The driving force behind Wakehurst Place is conservation and concerted efforts in the Wetlands and Loder Valley, and along the dramatic Rock Walk, for example, have resulted in national and international recognition.

MILLENNIUM SEED BANK

The Millennium Seed Bank is probably the most ambitious conservation project in the world and its interactive exhibition is a magnet for anyone wishing to learn more about plants and their intimate relationship to mankind.

What's in a name?

Plants are known by a variety of names. They have both common names and scientific or Latin names. However, the same plant may be called by a variety of common names in different places. This is obvious with overseas countries and foreign languages, but the same plant may also have different regional names in the same country. For example, here in the UK, bird's-foot trefoil (*Lotus corniculatus*) is also known as hen and chickens, Tom Thumb, granny's toenails, cuckoo's stockings, and Dutchman's clogs. But any botanist, from Aberystwyth to Zagreb, knows what is meant by *Lotus corniculatus*.

The advantage of the scientific name is that it is recognised everywhere. The advantage of a *Latin* scientific name is that as Latin is a dead language, it cannot change its meaning, but, at the same time, is very descriptive. There are no political or nationalistic overtones in Latin, either, so it is readily accepted throughout the world.

For the sake of easy reading, scientific names have generally been omitted from the main body of the text in this guide, in favour of common names where they exist.

FAMILY GROUPS

The basic group for plants is a *species*, with a unique combination of leaf, stem, flower, fruit and seed characteristics. Species are often found in a particular geographical area and don't usually interbreed. When species have general characteristics in common, they are themselves grouped into a *genus* (plural *genera*). Several genera with basics in common can be put into a larger group, called a *family*, such as 'grasses' or 'pines'.

RECOGNISING PLANTS

This typical label shows the system used within the Royal Botanic Gardens, both at Kew and here at Wakehurst Place. It refers to the giant Himalayan lily, illustrated left. Other plant labels may contain additional symbols or information.

Collector's or donor's code and plant's collection number

Accession number: a unique number given to each plant or group of plants in Kew's collection

Plant family

1975-6380	LILIACEAE
HADY	
"GIANT HIMALAYAN LILY"	
Cardiocrinum	
giganteum	
F	HIMALAYA, CHINA, JAPAN

When shown, N here states that the plant originated from wild source material

Plant's natural distribution range

Common name

F signifies that the identity of the plant has been verified by a botanist at Kew. (NB: on some labels, ● signifies the same thing; on others P signifies part verification.)

Scientific name shows genus and then species

Tony Schilling Asian

High in the mountains of Asia, the climate is so harsh that very few trees can survive. Plants here have evolved to resist extremes of temperature, rain and wind. The most common plants are the dwarf rhododendrons which are the equivalents of heathers on British moorlands. Growing among them - and familiar imports to these shores - are shrubs such as cotoneaster, potentilla, gaultheria and juniper.

The Tony Schilling Asian Heath Garden mimics a natural mountain habitat of rolling hummocky moorland with occasional areas of low woodland. The plants here are typical of the many types of mountain vegetation found in Asia.

The Summer House is more than a scenic shelter; it contains detailed information on Asian heathlands.

Westwood Valley (15mins)
Westwood Lake (30mins)

Heath Garden

Perhaps surprisingly, the Great Storm of 1987 had many positive aspects (see pp 84-85). It cleared the vast majority of the existing trees and rhododendrons in this area, enabling the garden to be created with a high degree of rationalisation and replanting. Specimens from the different mountain regions of Asia - those of Korea, the Sino-Himalayas, Taiwan and Japan - are grouped together in separate beds for more accurate representations of their native habitats.

SEASONAL NOTES

The dwarf rhododendrons are at their best in May, but the Asian Heath Garden has something of interest throughout the year and gives gardeners many ideas for plantings in exposed conditions.

TONY SCHILLING

Plant collector and landscape creator, Tony Schilling was responsible for the gardens at Wakehurst Place from 1967 to 1991. His passions were for the Himalayas where he worked and collected extensively, particularly with high-altitude rhododendrons. The Asian Heath Garden, named after him, and the Himalayan Glade (see pp 32-33) are recreations of the landscapes so familiar to him.

* *Rhododendron degronianum* subsp. *yakushimanum* is among the most spectacular you can find - a compact plant absolutely smothered with flowers, ranging from white, through pale to deep pink.

Sir Henry Price bought Wakehurst Place in 1936, having fallen completely for both the house and the gardens. Although their plans were interrupted by the Second World War, he and his wife, Lady Eve Price, restored the Mansion and continued to improve the gardens to the extent of becoming major exhibitors at Royal Horticultural Society Shows. Several award-winning plants were named after them, including *Viburnum* 'Eve Price' and *Pieris* 'Henry Price'.

One of the two walled gardens adjacent to the Mansion, the Sir Henry Price Garden is a fitting memorial to the man. Here, informal groups of plants have a decidedly 'cottage-garden' feel to them; the impact being heightened by the deliberate limitation to plants with foliage and flowers in pastel shades. The atmosphere is very restful, with grey and silver-leaved artemisias and lavenders providing a perfect foil for other species with pink, blue and lilac flowers.

As expected from a cottage garden, most of the plants are herbaceous perennials, but tender annuals are added to provide more interest within the overall colour scheme, while the shrubs give strength and structure to the design.

Pinetum (10 mins)
Horsebridge Wood and Rock Walk (30 mins)

Winter Garden
Slips and Water Garden (10 mins)

Look out for the herbaceous geranium garden which has a profusion of pink, mauve and blue flowers; and at the Mansion end, the silvery willow-leaf pear trees are very attractive and quite unusual.

Seasonal Notes

The Sir Henry Price Garden is at its colourful best during the summer months.

The secluded Pleasaunce Garden is entered directly from the Sir Henry Price Garden, each providing a tranquil complement to the other.

The Pleasaunce could be described as a garden within a garden, since the central small lawn with formal bedding and attractive ornamental fountain is itself contained within wonderfully clipped yew hedges, with dramatic arches that frame delightful portraits of the garden's features. The yew hedging was originally planted in the days of Sir William Boord (1890-1903).

Outside the yew hedges, but inside the outer walls, there are more flower beds, some filled with late summer-flowering shrubs, among which a bank of fuchsias is splendidly apparent, complete with a timely warning about the numbers of active bees. The walls themselves support rare climbing shrubs, such as the yellow-flowered honeysuckle, *Lonicera trogophylla*.

Pinetum (10 mins)
Horsebridge Wood and Rock Walk (30 mins)

> **SEASONAL NOTES**
> The formal Pleasaunce Garden
> has attractive bedding schemes for
> both winter and spring.

Slips and Water Garden (10 mins)

The massive yew hedge needs clipping only once a year, in August; yet because it grows so slowly, it keeps its geometric symmetry and precision. The dark foliage provides a marvellous background for the formality of the fountain and statue.

On the western side of the Mansion, the Winter Garden shows how to generate colour and interest in the drab months between November and February. There are some familiar names here, together with groupings of rarer plants that deserve to be better known. Brightly coloured dogwood and willow stems contrast with the shapes and colours of the dried leaves of ornamental grasses.

The Winter Garden also holds part of the National Collection of *Skimmia*, where their evergreen foliage and berries in the case of female bushes, contribute to the ornamental theme.

Horsebridge Wood (25 mins)
Rock Walk (30 mins)

Pinetum
Westwood Valley (15 mins)
Himalayan Glade (10 mins)

Specimen Beds
Slips and Water Garden (10 mins)

SEASONAL NOTES
As the name suggests, the Winter Garden is the place to come for ideas when much of nature is at a low ebb.

* The brightly coloured stems of the willows (*Salix*) and dogwoods (*Cornus*) put on an uplifting, vibrant show on even the gloomiest of days.

Adjacent to the Winter Garden, towards the walled gardens, the Monocotyledon Border is well worth careful study. Monocotyledons are plants with a single seed leaf (cotyledon). Many develop narrow parallel-veined leaves, such as lilies, grasses and red-hot pokers (*Kniphofia*). 'Monocots' on view range from common specimens such as narcissus to the unusual ginger-lilies (*Hedychium*) which grow well here.

> ### SEASONAL NOTES
> Always interesting, but the Monocotyledon Border is appreciated more for its midsummer colour.

Southern Hemisphere

One of the more popular parts of the gardens at Wakehurst Place, the rare plants of the Southern Hemisphere Garden make a significant impact on the local landscape.

Not so long ago, the question that taxed botanists was how, when the land masses of South America, southern Africa, Australia and New Zealand are separated by such vast tracts of ocean, did so many related species turn up so far apart? For example, members of the Proteaceae family are found in all four land masses, but never in the Northern Hemisphere. The theory of continental drift solved that problem, but nonetheless, Southern Hemisphere plants were a source of fascination to many, including Gerald Loder, who was responsible for starting Wakehurst's outstanding collection.

A photo opportunity not to be missed, looking back to the Mansion from the border of the Southern Hemisphere Garden.

SOUTH AMERIC
Embothrium coccii

SO_

*Eucaly_*

NEW ZEALA_
*Cordyline indivis_*

Garden

CONTINENTAL DRIFT

Some 120 million years ago, the southern continents were massed together (Gondwanaland) and many plants evolved there. Over the millennia, the continents drifted apart with the movement of their tectonic plates to their present positions, splitting up South America, Africa, India, Antarctica and Australia. Descendants of some of the original groups of flowering plants can still be found in parts of South America, Africa and Australia, separated by vast tracts of ocean.

The genus *Hebe*, well represented in this garden, was one of the few flowering plant groups that spread to the land that became New Zealand before it became isolated in the Southern Ocean and developed its own unique flora. Hebes have evolved to fill many ecological niches, from small shrubs to woodland trees. The garden also has a fine show of cortaderia, and a rare daisy bush *Olearia lacunosa*.

With painstaking care not to alter its visual impact, the Southern Hemisphere Garden is being rationalised into more distinct geographical plantings as found elsewhere in Wakehurst; the main groupings will become New Zealand, Tasmania, Australia, South America and South Africa.

CA
phofia

SMANIA
Banksia

TRALIA
iflora subsp. niphophila

In April and May, look out for the spectacular show of the waratah (*Telopea truncata*) with a big head of bright red flowers, carried right at the end of the shoots. For those tempted to try growing it, this plant needs acid soil.

SEASONAL NOTES
There is year-round interest in the Southern Hemisphere Garden.

The Specimen Beds and Na...

WAKEHURST PLACE IS HOME TO FOUR NATIONAL COLLECTIONS, BROUGHT TOGETHER IN THE BED NEXT TO THE STABLE RESTAURANT. SPECIMENS OF HYPERICUM (ALSO KNOWN AS ST. JOHN'S WORT) AND SKIMMIA CAN BE SEEN IN VARIOUS OTHER PARTS OF THE ORNAMENTAL GARDENS AS DESCRIBED BELOW.

Farm Walk

NATIONAL HYPERICUM COLLECTION

All hypericum flowers are created yellow, but some are more yellow than others. Most of Wakehurst's National Collection of hypericums dominate the Specimen Beds in July and August and range from the delicate primrose of *Hypericum bellum* to the familiar strong, glossy yellow of *Hypericum* 'Hidcote'.

The hypericum genus is a large one, with some 350 species found in the world's alpine, temperate and subtropical regions. They can be tree-like, as in East Africa's *Hypericum revolutum*, or tiny annuals.

The National Collection brings the opportunity to see lesser-known but very garden-worthy specimens, such as *Hypericum bellum*, which has a very attractive dense and compact habit, and finely-cut, slightly downy leaves with wavy margins; *Hypericum pseudohenryi* with its attractive pink-flushed stems; and *Hypericum subsessile*, which has rich red fruiting capsules in late summer. The collection is developing even greater representation of shrubby hypericums and also enhancing its genetic diversity with more material gathered from the wild.

Hypericum 'Hidcote'

Hypericum bellum

Hypericum dummeri

NATIONAL SKIMMIA COLLECTION

Wakehurst's skimmias are found throughout the ornamental gardens; some are in the Winter Garden, others by the Chapel and more along Farm Walk.

In the wild, skimmia comprises four well-defined species, all of Asian origin. The relationships of species in the genus were finally unravelled in the Herbarium at Kew after nearly a century of confusion. A great many of the skimmias currently in cultivation are represented at Wakehurst Place and have been accurately named.

With cultivars, accurate naming is still problematical, but the effort continues with, for example, 28 of the 53 known named cultivars of *Skimmia japonica* subsp. *japonica* having been identified. Of particular interest are the three known cultivars of *Skimmia* x *confusa*, which is the only genuine hybrid in the family; all of them are grown at Wakehurst Place.

THE GAZEBO, erected in memory of Peter Bowring (1913-90) has the outer framework planted alternately with laburnum and wisteria, flowering yellow and mauve, which were the Bowring horse racing colours.

National Collections were instigated by the National Council for the Conservation of Plants and Gardens (NCCPG) to conserve the rich garden flora of the British Isles, because many garden plants - particularly herbaceous perennials and annuals - were being lost from cultivation. By gathering all the species and cultivars of a plant family together, the scheme creates a comprehensive and accurately named resource for both conservation and reference. Interested individuals and organisations have access to National Collections through the NCCPG.

The four National Collections at Wakehurst Place are skimmias and hypericums described here; southern beeches in Coates Wood (see pp 54-57) and birches in Bethlehem Wood (see pp 58-59).

Mansion Pond &

Spring Border

The waterlily-filled Mansion Pond is an integral feature of the landscape of Wakehurst Place. The house is reflected in it and by virtue of its position, it connects many garden features. The Asian Heath Garden leads directly away from it and the Slips are viewed from the charming balustrade. An artificial rock outcrop is carpeted with low-growing perennials and the eye is drawn to some splendid Japanese maples, star magnolias and rhododendrons.

As with all water features, visitors need to take special care of children. Many recent plantings around the pond have been made specifically to take heed of Health and Safety regulations.

The Spring Border is one such planting and not only defines the limits of the open space, but also emphasises the background to the Mansion Pond, adding greater interest with some bold vertical accents in the form of *Sorbus* 'Dirkenii' and *Prunus* 'Ukon'.

> **SEASONAL NOTES**
>
> By definition, the Spring Border is alive with flowers from late March through to late May, and the nearby magnolias and rhododendrons start their show at this time.

Pinetum (10 mins)
Himalayan Glade (15 mins)

Slips and Water Gardens
Westwood Valley (10 mins)

* The Japanese maples at the north end of the Spring Border are noted for their great variety of shape, leaf form and autumn colour. The plants here predate Kew's role in the gardens and were probably added by Lady Price.

The Slips

The Slips is a steep-sided valley, with a stream running through it, leading from the formal arrangements near the Mansion down to the valleys and woodlands. It still retains the style that Gerald Loder put into his plantings - a series of interesting, but unrelated, trees and shrubs planted relatively closely together, showing his catholic taste and relaxed design sense.

At the Balustrade at the top of the Slips, there is a sundial erected in his memory, and that of his head gardener, Alfred Coates. On its base are some words by J. G. Whittier:

> *"Give fools their gold and knaves their power,*
>
> *Let fortunes bubbles rise and fall,*
>
> *Who sows a field or trains a flower,*
>
> *Or plants a tree, is more than all"*

Careful inspection of the stream reveals that it is an entirely artificial construction - an object lesson for some of today's more fanciful fibreglass runnels and waterfalls? Alongside, there are rich and varied plantings of magnolias, pieris and cornus.

The sundial by the Balustrade

Mansion and Exit *(10mins)*

Water Gardens *(5mins)*
Westwood Valley *(10mins)*

Viewpoint over Water Gardens
Compost area *(5 mins)*

WILD FLOWERS IN BLOOM

The Slips is designed as a wildflower meadow, so from early May, look out for the wild flowers, including the orchids (mentioned above right), at the top of the Slips - on the left looking back towards the Mansion.

ORCHID CONSERVATION

From April, wild flowers grow in the grass between the magnolias at the top of the Slips. They include two native orchids; the green winged orchid (*Orchis morio*) shown here, one of the earliest into flower, followed in May by the taller Jersey orchid (*Orchis laxiflora*). They were raised from seed at Kew as part of the Sainsbury Orchid Conservation Project and were the first to be successfully planted out from glasshouse to open garden. Kew is constantly learning more about how to introduce rare orchids back into suitable habitats.

SEASONAL NOTES

Excellent displays from spring through to October, with fine shows of spring daffodils and crocuses, while the magnolias and pieris are splendid in spring and early summer. Throughout the summer, real interest is maintained by a carpet of Mediterranean shrubs, including rock roses and Jerusalem sage.

* 2 WAKEHURST'S OWN PIERIS

Perhaps the most flamboyantly-leaved pieris is one which originated in these gardens, *Pieris formosa* var. *forrestii* 'Wakehurst', and the Slips is one of its many locations in the gardens.

27

Continuing downstream along the Slips, the next expanse of water is the Black Pond, which has also been known as Black Swan Pond, though none of those unusual birds are found there today.

After the Black Pond, the Ditch Beds are justifiably much-visited for the Himalayan blue poppies and giant Himalayan lilies whose presence cannot be ignored, either when in June flower, or later in the year when they produce massive sculptural seed heads.

Next comes the Iris Dell with its raised walkway and attractive seats, ideal for contemplating the calm of the central pond with water hawthorn and surrounded by irises, maples and rhododendrons. This peaceful haven is suffused with the sound of an elegant waterfall.

Following the water downstream still further takes the inquisitive visitor to the hidden charms of the Water Garden, with its mix of moisture-loving and woodland flowering plants.

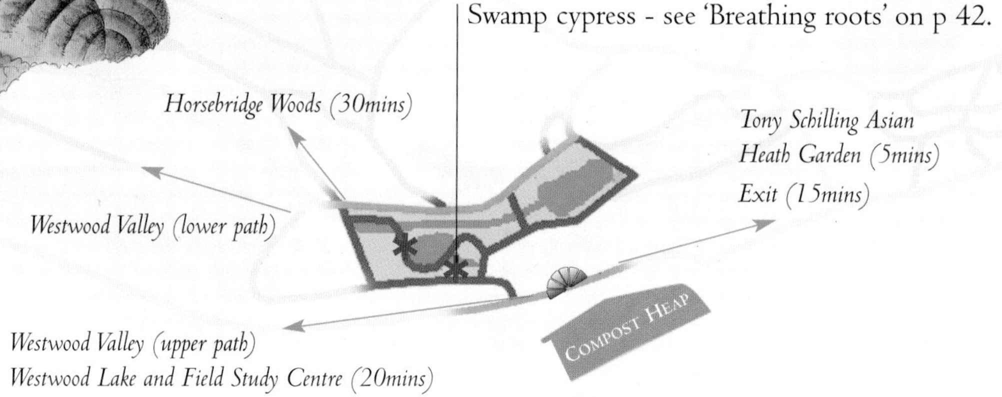

Swamp cypress - see 'Breathing roots' on p 42.

Horsebridge Woods (30mins)

Tony Schilling Asian Heath Garden (5mins)

Exit (15mins)

Westwood Valley (lower path)

Westwood Valley (upper path)
Westwood Lake and Field Study Centre (20mins)

COMPOST HEAP

Iris Dell

The summer display of the Japanese irises is unmissable, but it is also interesting to note the progress through the season of the giant Himalayan lilies as they grow, flower and form architectural shapes with seed heads later on in the year.

SEASONAL NOTES

Herbaceous plantings from May onwards, followed in June by giant Himalayan lilies, blue poppies and primulas. From September, look out for the seed heads of the Himalayan lilies and other plants, and the subtle tones of autumn colour.

COMPOST - HEAPS OF INTEREST

Peat - for years, every gardener's first choice for mulching or for soil improvement - is a rapidly dwindling natural resource and peat bogs an increasingly threatened wildlife habitat. Kew largely suspended the use of peat in 1989, even though peat replacement technology was then in its infancy.

Today, all prunings and fallen leaves at Wakehurst are composted and there is also a joint enterprise with Ashdown Forest to compost bracken. The forest removes the accumulation of years of bracken waste to help its heather regeneration programme and Wakehurst benefits from a ready supply of compost for mulching and soil improvement.

At home, well rotted farmyard or stable manure are excellent soil conditioners and fertilisers; and mushroom compost is a good substitute, except for rhododendrons. Peat-free soil improvers and potting composts are readily available, while bark chippings and coconut products make good mulches. Recycling garden debris and organic kitchen waste in compost-makers or wormeries is good for the garden and relieves pressure on landfill sites.

The Pinetum

Conifers were Gerald Loder's particular passion. As his collection grew, he realised his first Pinetum - a conifer plantation - on the southern side of the estate was too small. In the early 1920s, he expanded the collection by planting in its present position across the valley.

After his death in 1936, the area became neglected until, in 1965, vigorous thinning and clearing revealed some extremely rare and very large specimens. Conditions had suited them and the Pinetum was a place for 'champions' in the world of rare conifers.

The Pinetum was ravaged by the Great Storm of 1987, with some 80% of the trees destroyed. Its status as a conifer collection was questioned. But, since many conifers thrive at Wakehurst, and given their importance to the gardens and their economic and evolutionary significance as a plant group, the Pinetum was re-established.

Conifer woodland is the most extensive forest in the world, larger in area than even the tropical rainforest. In the Pinetum, the new plantings are grouped in geographical areas representing Europe, North America, Asia and the Southern Hemisphere, and show variations in the major groups of conifers, particularly firs and spruces.

Wakehurst Place was the HQ of the 1st Canadian Corps from January 1942 to October 1943. They were to defend the South Coast in the event of invasion and maintain contact with resistance units. They built a secret underground communications room entered from the Dog Kennel Pits quarry in the Pinetum and traces of radio aerials have been discovered hidden in trees.

Horsebridge Woods (15mins)
Bloomer's Valley and Rock Walk (30mins)
Millennium Seed Bank and Exit (60mins)

Mansion (10mins)
Exit (15mins)

Viewpoint over Himalayan Glade accessible to wheelchair users.

Water Gardens and Slips (15mins)

*

This flat-topped grassy mound is Gerald Loder's golf tee, from which he used to drive balls across into Westwood Valley. On it grows a conifer which fascinated him, a *Taiwania cryptomerioides*, which grows two types of foliage; the juvenile form looking like cryptomeria, or Japanese cedar, while the adult form changes to look like sequoiadendron, or redwood. Also known as the 'coffin tree' because of the excellent preservative qualities of its resinous wood, this rare tree grows under glass at Kew, but thrives in the milder conditions at Wakehurst Place.

The Himalayan Glade

(Please note: The Himalayan Glade itself is not suitable for wheelchair users, but it is included in this section of the guide, because the superb viewpoint from below the Pinetum is very accessible.)

Here, the Wakehurst landscape is carved out of uncompromising chunks of Ardingly sandstone and the Himalayan Glade is in a deep cleft, situated along the north side of Westwood Valley (see pp 36-39).

It represents the mountain vegetation of the Himalaya and China, planted with a deciduous berberis giving a fine display of flaming scarlet leaves in autumn. There is a seasonal stream running down the centre of the Glade and by it are bold displays of polygonums and euphorbias, together with splendid ginger-lilies.

Horsebridge Woods (15mins)
Bloomer's Valley and Rock Walk (20mins)
Millennium Seed Bank and Exit (40mins)

Wetland Conservation Area and
Westwood Lake (5mins)

The Himalayan Glade as seen from the Pinetum viewpoint. This is a favourite spot for bird-watchers, who are amply rewarded for a little patience.

*
THE TALLEST TREE AT WAKEHURST
This superb Douglas fir (*Pseudotsuga menziesii*) is approximately 43 m (140 ft) tall. There is around 27 m (90 ft) of trunk before the first branches appear. It can be seen from the viewpoint below the Pinetum and, better, from the stone seat on the opposite side of the valley, from where this photograph was taken.

Water Gardens and Slips (15mins)
Mansion (20mins)
Exit (30mins)

There are steps down into the Glade from the viewpoint, and the small effort in descending them is amply rewarded with yet another example of the creative planting talent of Tony Schilling, who was responsible for the gardens from 1967 to 1991. He collected avidly in those far mountains and among his introductions to Wakehurst are *Euphorbia schillingii*, *Populus glauca* and *Skimmia laureola* subsp. *multinervia*. The ginger-lilies *Hedychium* 'Tara' and *Hedychium* 'Stephen' are named after his children.

SEASONAL NOTES

Rhododendrons and wild flowers from May onwards, with berberis and polygonums showing especially well in autumn. The rose-red *Bistorta vacciniifolium* is a fine specimen, found on the rocks to the west side of the Glade. Shown here is *Rhododendron hodgsonii*.

Temperate woodlands

For over 150 years, Wakehurst Place evolved by combining ornamental plantings and exotic tree collections within native woodland, which consists in the main of English pedunculate oak. The result was a rich and mature, but random, collection of trees and shrubs.

The 1960s and 1970s saw a more focused collection rationale, concentrating on grouping trees and shrubs according to the areas of the world in which they grew - a *phytogeographic* system.

Work was progressing well, when the Great Storm of 1987 laid low thousands of fine specimens. On the surface, this was a huge tragedy, but there came about the realisation that, in the long term, this enforced clearance had paved the way for a series of tree collections which would be scientifically more important, more attractive to visitors and more relevant to Kew's emphasis on conservation and education.

During the winter of 1989-90 numbers of trees were transplanted throughout Horsebridge Wood to conform to the new layout - a considerable undertaking in itself - and six distinct areas came into being.

While drawing up fresh plans for other parts of Wakehurst's woodlands, 1990 brought another violent storm, causing yet more damage. The last decade, however, has seen the planting plans taking on more and more physical shape.

AROUND THE WORLD IN 80 MINUTES?

Today, a fit visitor to Wakehurst Place could probably stroll briskly round the world's temperate woodlands in 80 minutes, gaining strong impressions of how various regions look, if not how they *feel*, because many of their own local climatic conditions cannot be accurately reproduced here. The page opposite shows the layout of the woodlands.

Part of the strong appeal of Wakehurst Place is year-round access to all the woodlands so that seasonal pleasures such as autumn colour in the deciduous collection from the Appalachian Province (see p 46) are easily realised.

On the following pages, there is more information on each woodland area, which may be supplemented with specialised literature and leaflets available in the Shop.

of the world

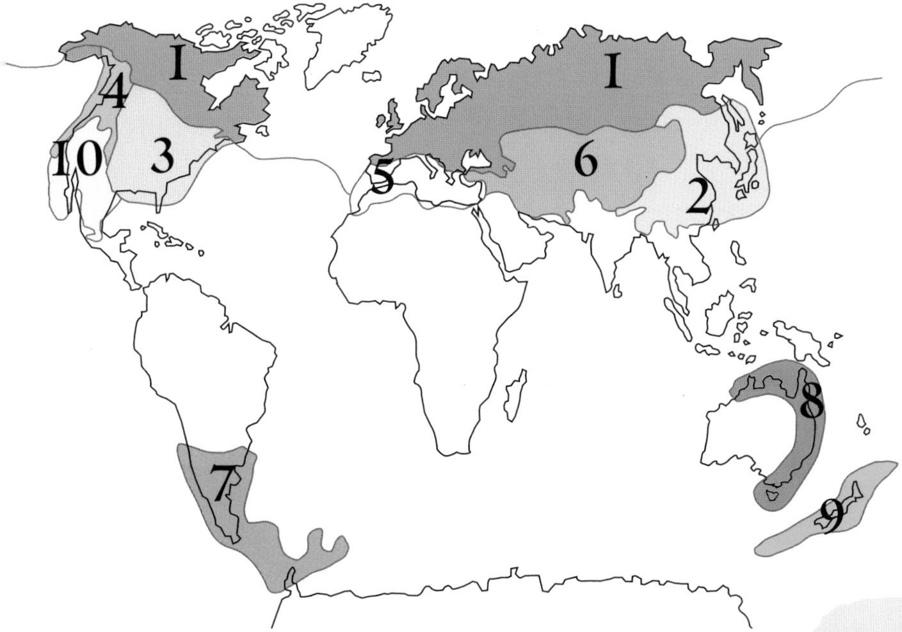

The map (left) shows the floristic regions of the world represented at Wakehurst Place. It is based on the widely-accepted phytogeographic classification of the eminent botanist, Armen Takhtajan (see p 84). Temperate zones stretch north from the Tropic of Cancer to the Arctic Circle and south from the Tropic of Capricorn to the Antarctic Circle, but temperate species also grow in cooler high places in the equatorial tropics. The diagram below locates representative tree collections from the various regions at Wakehurst Place. Visit Westwood Valley for the tree flora of eastern Asia; Horsebridge Wood for North American species; and all round Bloomer's Valley for Southern Hemisphere and Mediterranean trees.

1 CIRCUMBOREAL
2 EASTERN ASIATIC
3 NORTH AMERICAN ATLANTIC
4 ROCKY MOUNTAIN
5 MEDITERRANEAN
6 IRANO-TURANIAN
7 CHILE-PATAGONIAN
8 NORTH-EAST AUSTRALIAN
9 NEO-ZEYLANDIC
10 MADREAN

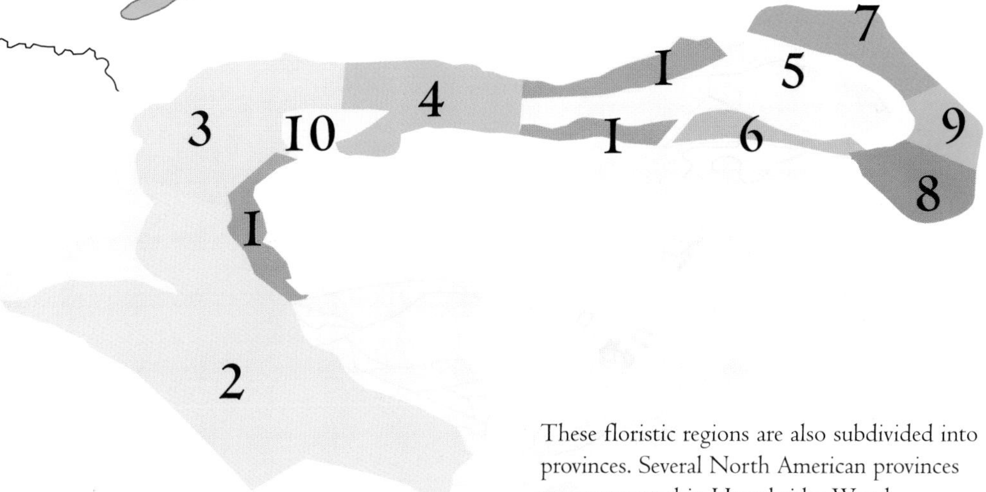

These floristic regions are also subdivided into provinces. Several North American provinces are represented in Horsebridge Wood (see pp 44-47).

Westwood Valley

The cool and moist growing conditions in the dramatic ravine of Westwood Valley make it an ideal home for the Asian collections at Wakehurst Place. The temperate regions of Asia, especially the eastern Himalayas, are the richest for plants, with over 4,000 species.

The fascination in which these plants are held by gardeners and botanists alike is that in many genera, or plant families, the choicest species almost always come from Asia - the most beautiful flowers, the most attractive bark, or the most vibrant autumn colour.

Eastern Asia was one of the major centres for the evolution of the very first flowering plants and conifers and species such as today's ginkgo and dawn redwood are found in fossils millions of years old.

The huge diversity of temperate woody plants in eastern Asia is because they escaped the advance of the glaciers in a protected area known as a *refugium*. There, they were able to adapt to an exceptionally wide range of

Bloomer's Valley and Rock Walk (20mins)
Coates Wood and Bethlehem Wood (30mins)
Millennium Seed Bank and Exit (40mins)

Southern Hemisphere Garden (15mins)
Mansion and Exit (25mins)

Water Gardens and Slips (5mins)
Mansion (20mins)
Exit (30mins)

BATS ABOUT BATS
Look for the bat roosts carved out
of dead trees in Westwood Valley,
and for bat boxes in Horsebridge
Wood. See pp 70-71 for more
about creating homes for these
charming and harmless protected
creatures.

conditions in a land mass ranging from
tundra to tropics; from high arid
mountains to lush valleys. Florida, in
south-eastern America, was another
refugium and there are many taxonomic
links between there and eastern Asia.

Westwood Valley represents the landscape
of the eastern Himalayas below the tree
line, with semi-evergreen forests of
rhododendrons, laurels, maples, alders,
oaks, birches and conifers. In particular,
the Valley's rhododendron collection is
being developed to show how these
glorious plants vary across Asia.

However, there are plants other than these
exotics in Westwood Valley. As befits a
wood in the Weald, there are natives here,
too - bluebells, lady's smock and the
common spotted orchid among them.

Westwood Valley

THE POPPY'S APPEAL

A single dried specimen of the Himalayan blue poppy (*Meconopsis betonicifolia*) was sent to Europe from China in 1886. However, it was not until Frank Kingdon-Ward sent the first seeds from the India-Tibet border in 1924, that this garden favourite could be grown in Britain. Of all the species of *Meconopsis*, with all their colours - red, blue, purple, yellow, orange and white - only one originates in Europe, the handsome Welsh poppy (*Meconopsis cambrica*).

SEASONAL NOTES

The rhododendrons in Westwood Valley are at their most spectacular in spring and early summer. The woodland floor is carpeted with bluebells in spring.

THE MYTH OF DAPHNE

Daphne was a beautiful daughter of the river god Peneus and the goddess Terra. Prompted by Cupid's darts, Apollo fell passionately in love with Daphne, but she was terrified and fled, calling upon the gods for help. They turned her into a laurel, whereupon Apollo made a crown of its leaves and declared that the tree should be evermore sacred to his divinity.

Daphne bholua (shown below) has superb displays of delicate highly-scented flowers from late winter through into March. *Daphne laureola* (spurge laurel) and *Daphne mezereum* are both British species. Spurge laurel is still used as a grafting stock for rare species.

RELATIVES, DRIFTING APART

The North American tulip tree is a close relative of the Chinese tulip tree but there are no tulip trees anywhere in between these two regions. Botanists believe that tulip trees evolved on land between Alaska and north-east Asia when the continents were closer together and the climates warmer. The flooding of the Bering Straits and advancing ice forced the original plants to migrate south, evolving into different, but closely related species in two vastly removed areas.

NATIVES AMONG THE EXOTICS

Two species of native helleborine, a group of hardy terrestrial orchids, grow in Wakehurst Place. They are the widely distributed broad-leaved helleborine (*Epipactis helleborine*) and the violet helleborine (*Epipactis purpurata*), which is found only in southern England. Other native orchids are the common twayblade (*Listera ovata*), with its yellowish-green flowers, which grows in dappled shade near the paths; and the spotted orchid (*Dactylorrhiza fuchsii*) shown above. See pp 26-27 about orchid conservation and reintroduction.

Westwood Lake and Wetland

There is water running all the way through Wakehurst Place. The streams from Westwood Valley and Horsebridge Wood have been dammed to create the attractive expanse of Westwood Lake, set in a valley and surrounded in the main by mixed native woodland.

Although artificial, the lake is more than a decorative feature. As well as being a useful habitat for local plants and animals, it is vital as a water store for the estate. One of the most frequently-asked questions is how the plants get watered and part of the answer is Westwood Lake. Alongside the path on the west side of the lake, the small building is a pump house, distributing water when needed to the many watering points on the irrigation system that runs throughout the gardens. Mains water from the public supply is never used to water the plants growing in the estate.

After Westwood Lake, the flow of water goes through the Wetland Conservation Area to Ardingly Reservoir and the Loder Valley Nature Reserve.

Bloomer's Valley and Rock Walk (20mins)
Millennium Seed Bank and Exit (40mins)

✳ ✳ BREATHING ROOTS - (see p 42)

Himalayan Glade (15mins)
Mansion and Exit via Pinetum (25mins)

 ✳ *Exit (40mins) via Slips and Water Gardens*

LODER VALLEY VIEWPOINT

Climb higher away from the Field Study Centre to find this superb viewpoint into the Loder Valley Nature Reserve.

Conservation Area

MEADOWS, WOODS AND WATER

Once, the Sussex Weald was a mixture of dappled woodlands, fragrant meadows full of grasses and wild flowers, and wetlands formed by a network of rivers, streams, lakes, ponds, marshes and ditches. As farming methods changed, meadows - and the plants that grew in them - became scarce. As flood control schemes drained land for more agriculture and urban development, wetlands decreased in area, too.

At Wakehurst Place, the typically Wealden geography with steep-sided ghylls and its combination of woodland, wetland and meadow makes it an important conservation area in south-east England.

In preserving these natural features, the Wetland Conservation Area and, more importantly, the Loder Valley Nature Reserve (described more fully on pp 66-67), offer a home for a rich diversity of native plants and animals.

UNWIND ON A KNOTTED SEAT

At the Loder Valley viewpoint, sit a while on the ornate knot design bench, designed and carved from quarter-sawn English oak by Will Glanfield. The form of the seat symbolises the endless motion and union of nature, while the legs depict two intertwining branches, one showing leaves of native trees, the other, leaves of exotic trees.

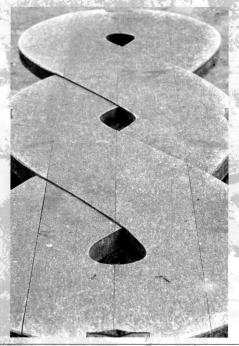

THE WETLAND CONSERVATION AREA

As entry to Loder Valley is restricted to 50 people each day, the Wetland Conservation Area in the south-west corner of the estate gives an easily-accessible flavour of the three main habitats.

The woodland is self-evident on either side of the paths to the Conservation Area. The wetland area is best seen from the raised walkway crossing an area of water and marsh planted with native water plants and marginals of all sizes, including reeds and, importantly, osiers - coppiced willows - whose shoots, when harvested, are used in basket-making.

Climbing away from Westwood Lake, a wide but steep path with an unmade surface reaches a small meadow, traditionally managed to allow the full flowering of grasses and wild flowers. This provides a habitat and food not only for small mammals and birds, but also for insects throughout their complete life cycle. Nectar plants are important for the adults, but their larvae often need different food plants.

At the back of the meadow is the SEEBOARD Field Study Centre designed for school parties and other students, and ideally placed for all types of ecological study. Its use is by prior arrangement.

BREATHING ROOTS

Where Westwood Lake meets Horsebridge Wood there is a naturally wet area, planted with a clump of swamp cypress (*Taxodium distichum*) from the south-eastern USA. Distinctive and characteristic of this tree are its pneumatophores. These are nature's snorkels, roots that come out of the glutinous mud in which the tree naturally lives to allow vital air into the root system. There is a swamp cypress with many easily-seen pneumatophores in the Iris Dell (shown here).

Conservation Area

BASKET CASES

The boardwalk in the Wetland Conservation Area crosses over beds of osiers, or withies; willows which are regularly cut back to ground level (coppiced) to harvest the new-grown thin, flexible, yet very strong shoots used in basket-making.

Horsebridge Wood

Coates Wood (15mins)
Millennium Seed Bank and Exit (40mins)

Wetland Conservation Area (10mins)
Mansion and Exit via Slips (45mins)

Himalayan Glade (10mins),
Mansion and Exit via Glade and
Pinetum (35mins)

Horsebridge Wood is a walk through North America. Much of pre-Columbian America was vast primeval forest. In the east, there were deciduous woodlands of oak, hickory and maple. In the north and west, conifers stretched for thousands of miles. The alluvial flood plains in the Gulf region and the south east suited pines and swamp cypress. The flat lands of southern Florida and the Caribbean islands were dominated by subtropical plants, such as coastal mangroves and, inland, palms, persimmons and evergreen oaks. When Europeans arrived, forest clearance for timber and agriculture began and today, there is very little of the old growth forest to be found.

Botanists divide North American forests into seven distinct provinces, based on their climates and the trees that grow in them. All are represented at Wakehurst Place except the subtropical West Indian Province, some of whose trees are grown in the conservatories at Kew.

In Horsebridge Wood, trees from the six provinces are planted not only in distinct areas (see the map key p 46), but where appropriate, species are also planted higher or lower on Wakehurst's slopes to represent their growing zones relative to each other in their homeland.

SCENIC ROUTE

To become more aware of the variety and sheer presence of some of these trees, it is worth while getting off the main tracks and heading up the slopes to walk the path by the deer farm.

Threatened bristlecone

On the path between Bloomer's Valley and Westwood Valley Lake, just by the fork to the Pinetum, there's a bristlecone fir (*Abies bracteata*), which has some of the longest needles of any fir. It is restricted to the Santa Lucia Mountains in California and, as a threatened species, it needs human intervention to help it survive.

Tall tales

After the Great Storm of 1987, only two mature coast redwoods (*Sequoia sempervivens*) were left standing in Wakehurst, though today, there are many more younger ones growing. The coast redwoods aren't as firm-rooted as the giant redwoods, which adapted to dry uplands with a wider spread of roots. They also bend more easily. Coast redwoods are among the world's tallest trees, with the tallest currently living being some 112 m (367 ft) high. There is some doubt as to which is the tallest tree species, as some of the south-western Australian mountain ash (*Eucalyptus regnans*) also grow to 100 m and more. Records from 1880 have a surveyor in Victoria measuring a standing tree at 114.3 m (375 ft) and another a trunk of a fallen tree at 132.6 m (435 ft) - possibly the tallest tree ever measured. Perhaps it can be simply agreed that *Eucalyptus regnans* are the tallest broad-leaved trees and *Sequoia sempervivens* are the tallest conifers.

Horsebridge Wood

The numbers in the boxes below refer to the floristic regions shown on the maps on p 35.

3 APPALACHIAN

Here, the Eastern deciduous woodland is justifiably famous for its 'Fall Colour'. There is also the widest variety of deciduous tree species in North America, with hickory, oak, maple and beech, joined by conifers at higher altitudes and to the north. The rarest tree in the province is the Virginia round-leaf birch, first discovered in 1914, then thought to be extinct until a stand of just fifteen trees was found in 1975. There is a specimen on the Birch Trail in Bethlehem Wood (see pp 58-59) - look for *Betula uber*.

10 CALIFORNIAN

Mild winters, hot dry summers - this climate is almost Mediterranean. Many of the plants here grow nowhere else in North America and even here in very restricted areas. The Monterey pine, for instance, is found in natural stands in only three places on the narrow coastal fringe between the mountains and the sea, yet it is one of the most valuable and widely-planted forestry trees, particularly in Southern Hemisphere countries such as New Zealand.

4 VANCOUVERIAN

All the way up the Pacific coast, from central California into Alaska, there's a continuous belt of coniferous forest. It thrives because the warm ocean currents just offshore make for mild winters and humid air, with plenty of rain, mist and fog. Some of the tallest and most massive trees in the world grow here, the coast redwoods, Douglas fir, sitka spruce and western hemlock.

3 GULF & SOUTH COAST

The poorer soils in this province are typically home to extensive pine forests which have adapted to frequent forest fires. Broad-leaved trees grow in areas which are lower and wetter, or higher places away from fire danger. There are a few conifers which are not evergreen, but deciduous. Swamp cypress is one of them and grows in this province, on flood plains and muddy river banks. See the feature on 'Breathing roots' on p 42 for more about the swamp cypress.

4 ROCKY MOUNTAIN

This province is mainly coniferous forest in which the mixture of species changes the higher up the mountains they grow. In the foothills, there's scrub oak and ponderosa pine. Then come the mountain and sub-alpine species, such as Engelmann spruce which thrives in cold humid conditions. In the Rockies, it grows right up to the tree line - the altitude above which no trees can grow - and is valued for its wood, much in demand for sounding boards in pianos and violins.

1 CANADIAN

This vast province stretches across the north of North America, from Alaska to Newfoundland, just south of the unforgiving frozen tundra plain. The harsh climate brings snow and ice for eight months of the year and the forests are dominated by conifers, with paper birch, quaking aspen and balsam poplar common on the southern flanks. Tamarack is an important tree in the north-western forest, for both its value to wildlife and its very durable timber.

3

BAT IN A BOX

Look out for bat boxes in Horsebridge Wood and for the bat roosts carved out of dead trees in Westwood Valley. Bat boxes don't have front entrances like bird boxes. Looking at the back-plate shows there are cross-cuts like a ladder, which the bat climbs up to slip through a tiny slot at the base of the box. See pp 70-71 for more about the bat protection and conservation programme at Wakehurst Place.

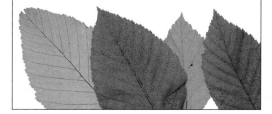

4

FALL FOR COLOUR

For autumn colour through Horsebridge Wood, there's a fine showing of the USA's east coast cherry birch (*Betula lenta*). When its leaves are pressed, they give out a strong smell of wintergreen.

NAME THAT TREE

In Britain, giant redwoods were called Wellingtonias, as what was thought to be a fitting tribute to the Iron Duke. However, the Americans had already named sequoias after Sequoyah (or George Guess), who was a renowned half-Cherokee scholar. Correctly, the coast redwood is *Sequoia sempervivens* and the giant redwood or Wellingtonia is *Sequoiadendron giganteum*. The trees are very closely related but the differences are clear, the giant redwoods being shorter, but more massive, with a more conical crown, and with very different foliage. Here, the giant redwoods are planted higher up the slopes to represent their altitude in nature.

Bloomer's Valley

Millennium Seed Bank and Exit
via Coates Wood (35mins)

Wetland Conservation Area and
Westwood Lake (20mins)

Westwood Valley (30mins)

Exit via Slips (60mins)

Bethlehem Wood and Birch Trail
Millennium Seed Bank and Exit
(20mins)

The sweep of Bloomer's Valley is an unexpected and very pleasant contrast to the wooded slopes all around it. Up until the 1960s it was planted with crops, but is now maintained as a swathe of frequently mowed open grassland.

The trees here are mainly from the Mediterranean and Irano-Turanian regions (see map on pp 34-35). The overall effect of the landscaping is enhanced by the contrast of tall specimens against the open expanse of the valley - an arrangement that has been described as like a cathedral and its piazza.

Many statuesque trees, such as cedars, pines and monkey puzzles, are shown to their best effect by this arrangement and plans are under way to enhance the dense woodland around the fringes of the valley, while allowing larger trees to emerge above the canopy.

Bloomer's Valley is most often viewed from one end or the other - when emerging from Horsebridge Wood or from the spectacular viewpoint high above the Valley in Coates Wood. However, exploration around the fringes, rather than a steady walk through, is very rewarding as there are some interesting and often important groups of trees here.

The Rock Walk (see pp 52-53) is often glimpsed from the floor of the valley and, with its outcrops of Ardingly sandstone, is an important feature in its own right.

MEET A PORCUPINE

On the northern side of the valley, just where the path forks up to Coates Wood, there's a rare type of porcupine fir (*Abies pinsapo* var. *tazoatana*) from northern Morocco. It was discovered by a Spanish forester working high up on the isolated Massif of Tazoat, who recognised it as one growing naturally in Spain. It is a close relative of the Moroccan fir from the Rif mountains and the Spanish fir from southern Spain.

Bloomer's Valley

RARE NATIVES

Up on the southern slopes of Bloomer's Valley, below the Rock Walk, is a collection of rare British native trees in the genus *Sorbus*. Among the 15 species are some familiar whitebeam, rowan and wild service trees, but also the Bristol mountain ash, rare in its native Avon Gorge. The rare Plymouth pear (*Pyrus cordata*), found in very few places in Devon and Cornwall, which is being conserved at Kew in the grounds of Queen Charlotte's Cottage, has also recently been planted in a group by the Millennium Seed Bank.

SEE THE CEDARS

The cedars in Bloomer's Valley are used as landscape statements. From these, and from others in the Pinetum, it is interesting to see the relationships and differences between the four species in the genus *Cedrus*. These are deodars from Afghanistan and Pakistan; Atlas cedars from north Africa; cedars of Lebanon from Lebanon and Turkey; and *Cedrus brevifolia* from Cyprus. Showing the great age some of these trees reach, cedars of Lebanon do not produce cones until they are between 40 and 100 years old. Western red cedar is not in this group as it is not a cedar, but a conifer from the genus *Thuja* found in western North America.

The Rock Walk

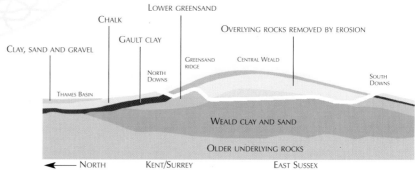

The Rock Walk is a path alongside a series of outcrops of Ardingly sandstone. Sandstone outcrops are a distinctive local geological feature of the High Weald and Wakehurst Place is fortunate in having over a kilometre of a typical rock face so prominently on view.

GEOLOGY OF THE HIGH WEALD

First formed in the Early Cretaceous period some 140 million years ago, from rivers depositing beds of sand and clay, the High Weald area was later covered by the Tethys Sea, which laid down more sand and clay, then a thick layer of chalk. After many sea retreats and land upheavals, south-east England eventually rose to form a huge dome stretching from the North Downs to France. The top of this dome gradually eroded first to remove chalk and then form the High Weald's inland sandstone cliffs. They are up to 15 m (50 ft) high and the majority are of Ardingly sandstone.

LOWER GREENSAND

CHALK

GAULT CLAY

OVERLYING ROCKS REMOVED BY EROSION

CLAY, SAND AND GRAVEL

GREENSAND RIDGE

CENTRAL WEALD

NORTH DOWNS

SOUTH DOWNS

THAMES BASIN

WEALD CLAY AND SAND

OLDER UNDERLYING ROCKS

← NORTH   KENT/SURREY   EAST SUSSEX

WAKEHURST'S ROCK WALK - AN SSSI
Wakehurst's massive sandstone outcrops, in mild shaded conditions with plenty of moisture, have promoted the luxuriant growth of a unique community of ferns, mosses, liverworts and lichens. The need to conserve these so-called 'lower plants' has resulted in the creation of the Wakehurst and Chiddingly Woods Site of Special Scientific Interest (SSSI), of which the Rock Walk is a prominent part.

Working in partnership with English Nature, Wakehurst's management of this site aims to protect and restore this important habitat by long-term monitoring of the changes that take place through conservation efforts, which include the clearing of the invasive *Rhododendron ponticum*.

Two key species being supported at Wakehurst Place are the slender-thread moss (*Orthodontum gracile*) and the veilwort (*Pallavicinia lyellii*). For more information on lichens, please see p 73.

✳ ROOTED IN THE PAST

A fantastical tangle of roots from yew, oak and beech writhes along some sections of the exposed face of the Rock Walk. Photographers will find their flash units useful or, better still, could shoot in natural light with the help of a sturdy tripod.

Coates Wood

Coates Wood, opened to the public in August 1977, is on land purchased from a neighbouring estate and named after Alfred Coates, a former head gardener at Wakehurst Place (see p 82). The original planting contained many fine conifers and significant hardwoods as well as the start of the southern beech collection, but whole swathes of trees were simply flattened in the Great Storm of 1987.

*Wetland Conservation Area and
Westwood Lake (30mins)*

Westwood Valley (40mins)

Mansion and Exit via the Slips (90mins)

*Bethlehem Wood and Birch Trail
Millennium Seed Bank and Exit (25mins)*

Nothing had prepared the estate for the ferocity of this storm, which was intensified by the venturi effect of the wind funnelling up Bloomer's Valley. The old and solid shelter belts originally planted by Gerald Loder were knocked flat.

Restoration work has progressed very well. Coates Wood is home to the superb National Collection of southern beech, or *Nothofagus*, from South America and Australasia, which grow well at Wakehurst. Both the *Nothofagus* and the other trees from Australia and New Zealand - mainly eucalyptus and broad-leaved evergreens - can dry out in winter winds and are liable to rock too much for the good of their roots.

Today, after weathering another severe storm in 1990, the team at Wakehurst Place knows a great deal about the design and planting of not only more effective shelter belts, but also the establishment of additional canopy cover.

The southern beeches, planted to represent a Southern Hemisphere temperate rainforest from Chile and Argentina, are in the western part of the wood.

Other specimens from New Zealand and Australia are planted in the eastern section. Interspersed among them are British native trees which have the dual purpose of

quickly establishing new woodland in cleared and damaged areas, and providing additional shelter for the Southern Hemisphere collections. Native oaks and ash are grown clear-stemmed to provide light for the southern trees, and form a protective canopy high enough to help protect them from damage by air frost.

* 2

PRIZE BEECHES WITH BIRCH BARK?

Among the southern beeches, there is one very rare semi-mature specimen of *Nothofagus glauca*, which has attractive peeling, varicoloured bark, much like birches. A very beautiful tree, it is claimed to be the UK champion of its species - a significant member of the National Collection. There are some younger ones close by, all grown from seed collected in their native habitat, which is in only one remote valley in northern Chile.

* 1

EUCALYPTUS TIPS

It's best for eucalyptus to make their first planting their only planting, since the young trees are susceptible to root rock and never do well if they are disturbed. Just by the featured shelter belt, there's a eucalyptus with three elegant and perfectly spaced trunks. It was damaged when young, so it was coppiced - the original trunk cut to about 30 cm (I ft) above ground level in April/May - and then three grew where one grew before. It is being allowed to mature.

Coates Wood

SHELTER BELTS - THEORY AND PRACTICE

Shelter belts are made from trees. Those at Wakehurst are designed not to stop wind completely - it always finds its way round or over obstacles and often creates even more damaging vortices in doing so - but to reduce its velocity significantly. That is the theory.

It works in practice. At this featured shelter belt, the planting is four rows wide, with the centre containing taller trees, so as to form a distinct 'A' shape. Overall, the ratio is two deciduous to one evergreen to allow the wind to pass through, but at a much lower speed, and therefore with less force.

The inner two rows consist of the deciduous whitebeam and Italian alder, which is a fast-growing nurse species to be rooted out after 20 years, and evergreens of Austrian pine and holm oak. The shrubs either side are yew, hawthorn, elder and holly. With this arrangement, the wind's speed is reduced and its direction taken upwards and away from the tender trees nearby.

This description is of a particular shelter belt near the Rock Walk which is a Site of Special Scientific Interest (SSSI) and so the species used for the shelter belt had to be approved by English Nature, who are responsible for the regulation of SSSIs in England.

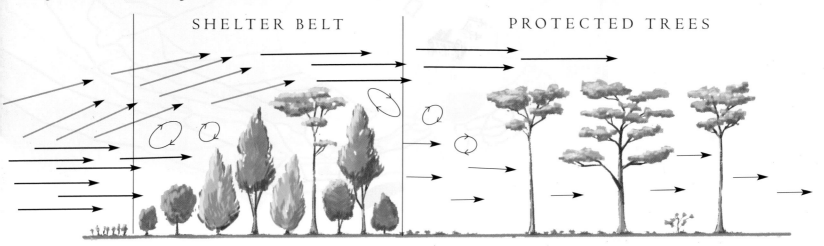

SHELTER BELT   PROTECTED TREES

TREE OR SHRUB?

When does a shrub become a tree? The word 'tree' instantly conjures up a picture of what it means, but the definition can be quite loose. Botanists usually agree that 'trees' are plants over 3-4 m (10-13 ft) tall, with a single clear woody stem that lasts for years, and with a branched crown. Shrubs generally have a characteristic tangle of branches and no discernible central stem. These characteristics can be readily seen in the planting of the featured shelter belt, very typically with the tall alder trees and compact elder shrubs.

Bethlehem Wood

Wetland Conservation Area and
Westwood Lake (30mins)

Westwood Valley (35mins)

Mansion and Exit via Slips (90mins)

Millennium Seed Bank (10mins)

Exit (20mins)

1

NORTH AMERICA'S RAREST TREE?

The Virginia round-leaf birch (*Betula uber*), once thought to be extinct. Cultivating these trees at Wakehurst helps ensure the survival of the species.

Bethlehem Wood is virtually exclusively devoted to its National Birch Collection. There are over 340 birches growing here, which is as comprehensive a collection as possible with the local growing conditions. It is best visited with the help of the Birch Trail leaflet, available from the Shop.

More than three-quarters of Wakehurst's birches have been raised from seed harvested in the wild in various parts of the world, when detailed notes of their growing conditions are made. Those records, together with the living specimens here, are used to study the distribution and relationships between species.

There are over 50 species of birch trees and shrubs growing in their native northern temperate and Arctic regions. Three are native to the British Isles; the silver birch, the downy birch and the dwarf birch.

Silver birch   Downy birch   Dwarf birch

(Leaves shown not to scale)

2

SISTERS UNDER THE SKIN
The colour of birch bark and the way it peels are striking family characteristics, but they can be influenced by the tree's environment, especially by differences in the soil, so it is not always possible to identify a birch species reliably by bark alone. For example, there are two Himalayan birches next to each other on the Birch Trail, of the same species, but with very different bark.

Birches are beautiful, with wonderful bark colours ranging from creamy-white, apricot and cinnamon to dark cherry-red and even chocolate. The whiteness comes from betulin, the wax produced by birches, and the more the betulin, the lighter the colour. With such colour always on view, from bark to autumn foliage, birches are deservedly popular in small gardens throughout the country.

Birches are also economically important, their wood being used from turnery and furniture to flooring and plywood. Extracts are used in insecticides, snakebite remedies and wintergreen, and native peoples in North America traditionally used the bark from the paper birch to make paper, baskets and canoes.

They are important as 'pioneer' species, too, being among the first trees to colonise areas where vegetation is cleared. This is because they are very hardy and able to tolerate inhospitable soils, are easily pollinated by the wind and distribute their seed efficiently.

3

MAGIC CARPETS
Bethlehem Wood has a magical carpet of primroses and ladies smock in early spring and later, around May, bursts into a sweeping show of bluebells. There are more bluebells all the way through Horsebridge Wood.

The Millennium Seed

The aim of the Millennium Seed Bank Project is to conserve biodiversity by storing the seeds of not only every native plant in Britain, but equally importantly, those of some 24,000 other species from around the globe.

It is probably the most ambitious conservation project in the world. Its interactive exhibition gives fascinating insights into plants and their intimate relationship to mankind.

Seeds have an astonishing ability to cling on to life against incredible odds. They'll certainly survive the dry sub-zero conditions in the Millennium Seed Bank vault. Visitors to the exhibition will learn:-

Why Kew started this international project and its importance to future generations

How seeds are collected in the wild

How the laboratories and seed preparation areas go about their work

How the vaults will safeguard 24,000 plant species for hundreds of years.

The £80 million project was part funded by the Millennium Commission and supported by the Wellcome Trust and Orange plc, together with many other organisations and individuals. The Royal Botanic Gardens, Kew would also like to thank both the National Trust and MAFF (now DEFRA), without whose support, this idea would not have turned into the splendid and vitally important reality it has become.

Bethlehem Wood and Birch Trail (10mins)
Bloomer's Valley (20mins)
Horsebridge Wood (30mins)
Wetland Conservation Area and Westwood Lake (40mins)
Westwood Valley (45mins)

2 (p 65)

1

Mansion (10mins)
Slips (25mins)

Exit (5mins)

Bank

AT THE HEART OF THE PROJECT

The Wellcome Trust Millennium Building is named after the Wellcome Trust, one of the world's premier medical charities, who have donated over £9 million in recognition of the importance of plants as sources of medical benefit.

LITTLE AND LARGE

The wide range of seeds on show in the main display area, the Orange Room, reflects the diverse ways which plants have developed to distribute their seeds to ensure the survival of their species on earth. They range from tiny seeds that fly on the wind to the largest seed in the world, that of the double coconut palm from the Seychelles, which can spend months at sea before washing up to grow on a new shore. Many seeds are inside fleshy fruits which provide food for birds and animals. These are carried away in, and later passed out of, the stomachs of the creatures that eat them. Delicious and nutritious fruits are a highly effective method of attracting animals to disperse the seeds they contain.

Illustrated here are the seeds of the double coconut palm (*Lodoicea maldivica*) at $\frac{1}{12}$ actual size, and a phial of the miniscule seeds of the lady's slipper orchid (*Cypripedium calceolus*). At only 100-200 cells in size, they are smaller than a full stop on this page. By comparison, a double coconut seed can measure up to 40 cm (16 in) long by 80 cm (32 in) diameter and weigh 20 kg (44 lb).

The Millennium Seed

WHY CONSERVE?

Plants are essential to people. They provide food, fuel, fibres, medicines and much more. Today, natural environments are being destroyed so quickly, so comprehensively, that it is not always possible to conserve plants in their own habitats. The next plant to become extinct might be the source of an important medicine. The only effective and economical alternative is to save seed and store it in seed banks. Large quantities of seeds are collected and stored to last possibly hundreds of years. When and if they are needed in the near or distant future, the seeds will be germinated, to reintroduce plants to the wild, or be used in scientific research to find new ways of benefiting mankind.

DOES IT WORK?

Kew scientists have germinated some of the very first seeds placed into the then highly experimental seed bank at Wakehurst Place back in 1974. After 25 years, cock's-foot grass (*Dactylis glomerata*) sprouted at the first attempt. With some 95% of our native wild plants safely banked, Britain is the first country to have harvested and preserved its botanical heritage.

Those seeds that cannot be banked in this way - acorns and sycamore keys for example - are being studied to find out why they don't survive drying and to investigate alternative long-term storage techniques.

PARTNER COUNTRIES

Key to the success of this conservation initiative is the participation and collaboration of other countries. To date, Burkina Faso, Kenya, Madagascar, Lebanon, South Africa and USA have signed agreements, and discussions at various stages are taking place with many other countries, including Australia, Canada, China and Zambia.

Since 1997, expeditions have taken place in the Middle East, Africa, the Americas and elsewhere. Some of the seeds collected are stored in the Millennium Seed Bank, the rest are kept in their countries of origin. The seeds stored here will be made available to researchers, conservationists and scientific institutions, free of charge. Under written agreements, a proportion of any benefits arising from the use of the seeds is returned to the country of origin.

Bank

SOWING SEEDS OF KNOWLEDGE

An important aspect of the Millennium Seed Bank is passing on Kew's expertise in seed conservation to other countries, especially those in the tropics. A good deal of the seed processing and research is carried out by visiting scientists working on their own native flora - work in which they are trained and assisted by Kew staff.

By encouraging visits to the Millennium Seed Bank with its interactive exhibits, Kew is undertaking another vital aspect of its task; that of public education. The importance of plants to people cannot be overstressed. It is no exaggeration to say, quite simply, that all human life depends on plants. Conserving plant seeds is a way of helping to preserve human life. It really is as simple and as important as that.

The Millennium Seed

The exterior features around the Millennium Seed Bank are exceptionally interesting, too. The landscaping is designed to reflect English native landscapes in the selection of trees and shrubs. All plants are sourced locally and the plantings of traditional hedgerows and small woodland blocks combine with sloping grassy banks on which there will be shows of wild flowers. Also, among the oaks, there are some rare Plymouth pears which are being conserved for the future here, in Bloomer's Valley and at Kew (see p 50).

The eight habitats are:

BED 1: Shifting shingle – plants of shingle beaches.

BED 2: Precarious positions – plants of cliff faces.

BED 3: From sheep to scrub – plants of chalk downland.

BED 4: Making hay – plants of meadows.

BED 5: Into the mire – plants of fens and marshes.

BED 6: In retreat – plants of the hills and mountains.

PARTERRES PAR EXCELLENCE

Outside the building, a growing source of interest are the eight parterres constructed and planted to represent habitats under threat. Four beds mimic the growing conditions of threatened habitats between the Sussex coast and Wakehurst Place. The other four demonstrate habitats threatened elsewhere in the United Kingdom. Each parterre contains soil appropriate to the habitat it represents but carefully adapted to its situation in a raised brick bed. One further bed in the Orange Room represents dryland plants from all parts of the world. The grasses and other plants that grow naturally in each habitat have been raised from seed gathered in the wild and, as well as growing here, are conserved in the Seed Bank vault.

Bank

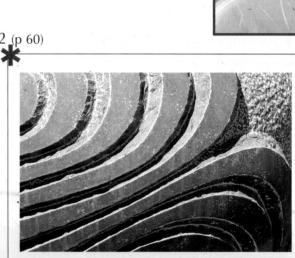

2 (p 60)

BED 7:   A burning issue – plants of heathlands.

BED 8:   Vanishing weeds – plants of cornfields.

There is one further bed, found in the Orange Room:

BED 9:   A global threat - the interior planter. This represents
             dryland plants from all parts of the world.

SCULPTED SEEDS

The sculptures outside the Millennium Seed
Bank are the work of Peter Randall-Page, who
lives and works in Devon, and is fascinated with
the forms and shapes of the natural world.
Carved from Kilkenny limestone and each
weighing around 2.5 tonnes, they capture the *idea*
of seeds, rather than specific seeds. The sculptor
has described seeds as being like "unexploded
grenades of life force" and in the abstract swirls
and whorls of the designs he created, that force
seems about to break out to germinate. As a
sedimentary rock, Kilkenny limestone is full of
tiny fossils - perhaps a symbol of the millions of
life forces stored in the vaults of the Millennium
Seed Bank itself.

The birds in Wakehurst's gardens are remarkably tame and chaffinches, robins and even pheasants feed from the hand. Broods of mallards and moorhens take up residence on the ponds and lawns around the Mansion, which also see pied wagtails and the occasional grey heron. Some birds breed in the grounds and stay all year; others are migratory visitors, such as the swifts in the Mansion eaves which winter in southern Africa.

In the Pinetum, greenfinches, goldcrests and siskins are regular visitors and hawfinches are occasionally spotted. Park and woodland birds, such as coal tits, marsh tits and nuthatches may be seen from the Himalayan Glade viewpoint. Nuthatches can walk vertically down tree trunks, while treecreepers look for food walking upwards.

From Westwood Lake and out into the Loder Valley Nature Reserve, grey wagtails and kingfishers are welcome sights.

Cormorants roost on Ardingly Reservoir, where great crested grebes regularly breed and where sandpipers feed on their migrations.

The woods and parklands are home to woodcocks, tawny and little owls and other birds of prey, including sparrowhawks and kestrels, with frequent sightings of hobbies and ospreys in the Reserve. The coppiced cover is used by warblers migrating from Africa, with arguably the most beautiful song coming from the blackcap.

LITTLE OWL

KESTREL

GREY HERON

CHAFFINCH

GREENFINCH

COAL TIT

NUTHATCH

ROBIN

WILLOW WARBLER

GREY WAGTAIL

PHEASANT

OSPREY

MALLARD

GREAT CRESTED GREBE

TAWNY OWL

68

DRAGONFLY OR DAMSELFLY?

The difference between dragonflies and damselflies is easily seen at rest. Dragonflies keep their wings outstretched, while most damselflies fold theirs back along their bodies.

The flying stage is the very last part of their lives, concerned mainly with reproduction. Eggs are laid either into plant tissue (under or near water) or directly into the water. When they hatch, the nymph stage can last several years in some species. The carnivorous nymphs have fierce prey-seizing jaws on an extendible 'mask', a feature unique to dragonflies and damselflies. They feed on insects and other small creatures, but some, like the Emperor dragonfly nymph, are able to take small fish.

Mature nymphs crawl up plant stems into the open air for their final moult, when the adult flying form emerges, waiting for wings to expand and legs and body to harden before searching for food and a mate.

Some 20 species of dragonfly can be seen at Wakehurst, about half of the total occurring in Britain. At Wakehurst, they

Brilliant Emerald dragonfly   Red-eyed damselfly

find the vegetation they need, as some grass areas close to ponds are deliberately left uncut as feeding sites, and elsewhere, trees are pruned to increase the sunlight needed for water plants. A good observation point is the board walk over the reed beds in the Wetland Conservation Area (see pp 40-43).

BUTTERFLY OR MOTH?

There is no one single difference between all butterflies and all moths, but their antennae are a good guide. All British butterflies have little clubs or knobs at the end of their antennae, while all British moths but one don't. The exception is the burnet moth family, which don't look like typical butterflies and are generally sluggish fliers.

Thirty-three of the estimated 58 species of British butterfly have been recorded at

Wakehurst Place. Nectar plants are important for the flying adults, but food plants for their caterpillars are just as vital, together with proper habitat management to allow each species to complete its annual life cycle. The mowing regime of many areas is designed specifically to provide nectar for the adults and sufficient food to see the caterpillars through to their pupal forms.

Wakehurst's butterflies and moths are present at some stage of their life in winter, too. Some hibernate as adults, others as caterpillars or pupae, while the remainder overwinter only as eggs. In summer, they are all out, dividing their time between eating and trying to produce the next generation.

Animal life at Wakehu

Wakehurst Place works closely with local and national conservation groups to develop management techniques that benefit wildlife and, of course, provide the essential habitats to ensure they thrive.

CAUTION: DORMOUSE - HANDLE WITH CARE

Wakehurst is enthusiastically helping English Nature's Species Recovery Programme for the hazel dormouse. Ranking high in charm, this small, furry and pretty creature lives on insects, seeds, nuts and berries such as hazel and bramble. In autumn it gorges itself to build up fat reserves for winter hibernation. Coppicing parts of the woodland on a 10-15 year cycle lets hazels produce nuts and brambles grow, so providing both the dense cover and the food supplies the dormouse needs. Carefully sited nesting boxes are used to monitor the local population and help build up a national picture. Handling a dormouse is a skilled and delicate matter and handlers must be licensed.

BADGER IN THE WILD WOOD

Badgers are shy nocturnal creatures, emerging from their setts at twilight. They are surprisingly big, with powerful claws used for foraging and for digging the maze of underground tunnels and chambers in which they live. Setts are regularly cleaned and some have been in existence for hundreds of years. Badgers live in groups of six to eight adults according to their size of territory and the availability of food.

In late autumn, badgers line their nest chambers with layers of dead leaves which generate warmth as they gradually decay. The main sett is used for breeding, and although badgers mate throughout the year, their young are usually born in February, since the embryos are kept in 'suspended animation' until the best time for survival.

Cubs start to emerge in late April or early May, ready for their first playful rough and tumbles as they learn to fend for themselves.

Wakehurst's woodlands are ideal badger country. Badger-watching is a delight and is occasionally organised by prior appointment though the Loder Valley Nature Reserve booking procedure.

BOXING CLEVER WITH BATS

Bats are protected creatures, suffering in Britain from loss of habitat. The removal of the dead and hollow trees where they live in commercial forestry has contributed to the decline in numbers of some bat species. At Wakehurst Place, the storms of 1987 and 1990 did little to help the resident bat population, because dead and hollow trees blew down and other hole-dwelling creatures such as squirrels and starlings competed for the same territory, forcing the bats out of many remaining suitable sites.

Wakehurst's policy is to leave many dead trees standing, to decay and provide homes for the bats. But nature is often given a helping hand. In Westwood Valley, chainsaws have carved out sections of trunk from hollow trees. The sections are trimmed to make an access space and replaced (see p 37).

In Horsebridge Wood, bat boxes have been put up. These resemble bird boxes except there is no hole in the front. Instead, careful

inspection reveals a narrow access slit at the base of the box, up against the backplate. Look carefully and crosscuts can be seen, providing a 'ladder' for the bat to climb (see p 47).

WAKEHURST'S BAT SPECIES

Bats are among the world's most successful groups of mammals, with over 1,000 species, though most are now in decline due to habitat pressure. There are 30 species in Europe, of which up to 15 are found in the UK.

All British bats are insect-eating - no fruit bats and certainly no vampires - and belong to two families, the vesper or evening bats, and horseshoe bats, which are very rare and live in the south west.

Wakehurst Place is home to eight species and the gardens, lakes and woodland provide perfect habitats. Most roost in trees, but the common pipistrelle and serotine bats prefer to live in buildings and so are often seen around the Mansion and outbuildings.

BATS AT WAKEHURST PLACE

Pipistrelle
Noctule
Daubenton's bat
Brown long-eared bat
Whiskered bat
Brandt's bat
Serotine
Natterer's bat

The noctule flies high above Horsebridge Woods hunting for large insects; while the brown long-eared bat forages among the birch trees in Bethlehem Wood. Westwood Lake, with its great profusion of insects, is a popular feeding ground, especially for Daubenton's bat, hunting just above the water. This diversity of feeding strategy makes bats successful and able to live together. Above Westwood Valley, colonies of noctule and Daubenton's bats roost in the same beech tree.

Fungi - crucial to life

Fungi are neither plants nor animals, but a separate and highly diverse kingdom, found everywhere and essential to all life on earth. Many fungi are microscopic and include moulds and mildews. However, the most familiar are the larger fungi; mushrooms, toadstools, brackets and fairy clubs, which appear in the autumn on tree trunks and branches, rotting vegetation and soil. These are the fruit bodies of the fungus and are usually short-lived. The main body of a fungus consists of microscopic threads (*hyphae*) forming a network (the *mycelium*), that expands out through, and feeds on, organic matter by producing digestive enzymes to break it down.

Fungi are usually the primary decomposers in their habitats, and are immensely important for releasing and recycling essential nutrients and, in so doing, reducing organic bulk. Without fungi, the world would be buried under a mountain of plant debris.

At least 80% of all plants grow in mutual association with fungi and without their partner fungus within their root systems - a *mycorrhizal* association - many will either grow poorly or not grow at all. The fungus mycelium extends out well beyond the roots of the host plant, gathering nutrients for the plant to absorb and obtaining sugars from the plant in return. Most orchid seeds are so tiny that they contain no food reserves for themselves and cannot succeed unless the right fungus is present to provide their nutrition.

Mycology at Kew

It is estimated that more than 1.5 million species of fungi exist worldwide, but no more than 5% have been described. Scientists at Kew are studying fungi from around the world, identifying, describing and classifying them. They are also investigating their practical uses as biological control agents against pests such as insects and eelworms, with the objective of reducing the use of toxic pesticides. There is a wealth of information on 'mushrooms' in the Kew web site.

LOOKING AT LICHENS

Lichens look simple, yet biologically they are quite complex, consisting of two unrelated organisms - a tightly packed fungal tissue, with algal cells embedded in it. The fungi depend on their algal partners for the energy the algae fix through photosynthesis and in return, the algae are protected from drying out and have ready access to the nutrients that the fungus obtains. This is known as a *symbiotic* relationship, meaning 'living together'. It is a highly successful partnership, with around a fifth of all known fungi forming lichens.

The ability of lichens to cope successfully with inhospitable environments allows them to colonise even the most extreme habitats. For example, they are among the first colonisers of newly-formed rock - some even specialising in recently cooled volcanic ash and lava, highly toxic to most other organisms. At Wakehurst Place, there are various lichens growing on the acidic sandstone of the Rock Walk (see pp 52-53).

Some species, on the other hand, grow only on trees. The species present depend on the acidity of a tree's bark, with fewer species on the more acidic trees. Oak has highly acidic bark and so harbours fewer lichens than, say ash, which is much more alkaline. There are some ash trees with an impressive lichen cover near the toilet block by the Winter Garden and Monocotyledon Border.

Woodland management

Bad forestry gets bad press. Good woodland management, on the other hand, gets little publicity at all, in spite of the fact that it is an important economic and ecological force. Until early this century, Britain's woodlands supplied everyday items such as baskets, furniture, fencing, tools and fuel. As mass production using metals and plastics grew commonplace and wood was replaced by fossil fuels, woodlands became neglected, resulting in a steep decline in some plants and animals.

BALANCING OPPOSING OBJECTIVES

Wakehurst's woodlands are managed in the traditional way and demonstrate a sustainable, successful method of balancing the opposing objectives of maximising economic benefit while conserving a rich biological heritage.

Traditional woodland management, crafts and products are far from old-fashioned. They now lead a thoroughly modern movement to help rural economies and conservation. Complete non-intervention is also recognised as a valid conservation technique.

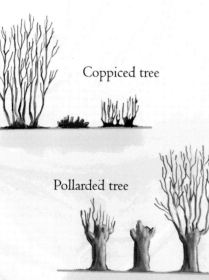

Coppiced tree

Pollarded tree

COPPICING - SHORT CUT TO SUCCESS

With coppicing, a tree is cut to the ground for one use; then the shoots that spring from its trunk and roots are harvested for other uses. Pollarding is coppicing, but higher up the tree, to prevent animals grazing on the new growth. Both methods treat tree shoots as a crop which not only satisfies particular needs, but also benefits the woodland by letting in light and allowing undergrowth to create an important wildlife habitat. Here, too, is where bluebells, wood anemones, primroses and violets really flourish.

HAZEL coppicing every 7-10 years produces pea sticks, bean poles, thatching spars, hurdles and fuel.

SWEET CHESTNUT is coppiced every 15 years for fencing. Other native species that can be coppiced include alder, beech, birch, field maple, small-leaved lime, sycamore, willow and wych elm.

HARDWOODS such as oak are coppiced on a 25-35 year cycle for charcoal production. Hardwood charcoal is excellent for its high carbon content; easy to light and quick to reach cooking temperature.

REBIRTH OF COUNTRY SKILLS

The rebirth of country style and increasing interest in rural matters has led to a rebirth of country skills.

Trugs use ash or chestnut frames and cleft willow for strength and lightness in the body.

Hazel hurdles are particularly strong, light and portable. Originally used for sheep folds, they are now fashionable garden screens.

Hay rakes in ash wood are naturally strong, yet light and resilient. They are still used by garden contractors, sports clubs and local authorities.

Bodgers are back, using simple pole-lathes made on the spot in the woodland to turn chair legs and spindles, shown here.

Tent pegs in ash or beech are not only strong, but have an inherent ability to grip the ground far better than metal pegs.

– a living resource

Besom brooms (above) are becoming more popular in country and town alike for their efficiency and traditional good looks.

Willow baskets have long played an important role in many rural economies and basket-weaving is practised by many craftspeople following patterns unchanged for centuries.

CHARCOAL PRODUCTION

Charcoal is used in Britain for domestic barbecues, in fireworks and in medicinal biscuits. Because of its ability to absorb gases and impurities, it is also used in chemical, water and vodka filters. Every year, some 60,000 tonnes of charcoal are sold in the UK, of which two-thirds are for barbecues. Only 3% (1,800 tonnes) is produced in Britain, yet there are huge supplies of low value wood available - an estimated 80,000 tonnes in south-east England alone. Sadly, much of what is sold is harvested unsustainably from tropical forests and mangrove swamps.

Charcoal is made by heating wood without enough air to burn it completely into ash. Wakehurst's portable steel kiln is moved around from coppice to coppice and is filled with carefully-arranged logs. A little wood is burnt

in the kiln to get it to working temperature and then, when the lid is put on and sealed, water boils out of the remaining wood, along with volatile tars and oils; leaving charcoal of up to 90% carbon. If air-dried wood is used, with a moisture content of less than 30%, then 4 tonnes of wood produces 1 tonne of excellent quality charcoal. Wakehurst produces and sells 3 tonnes of charcoal a year, the profits going back into conservation work.

Buying British hardwood charcoal, such as the Wakehurst-produced Bar-B-Kew brand, is the only way to be sure that imported wood from endangered tropical forests or mangrove swamps is not being used.

BAR-B KEW charcoal

ROYAL BOTANIC GARDENS KEW

English Hardwood Charcoal produced by traditional skills from sustainably managed coppiced woodlands at Wakehurst Place

Wood in the world

Wood is so much a part of everyday life that it can be taken for granted, but from earliest times, wood has been of great significance. Living trees were granted different qualities, often inhabited by spirits with magical powers. Dead trees were the source of light, heat and shelter, of totems, transport and weapons. Forests were both hunting grounds to provide food and mystic places generating a rich fund of folklore and fairytale. Even today, trees, woodland and forests have a powerful emotional effect on many people.

THE WAKEHURST BOG OAK

In 1976, when the Ardingly Reservoir was being constructed, a large piece of bog oak was unearthed from 4m (13 ft) below the surface and presented to the Wakehurst estate. It now lies in Hanging Meadow, carrying a plaque commemorating the opening of the Loder Valley Nature Reserve in 1980.

Bog oak is oak that has been preserved in wet airless conditions. It is often found in East Anglian fens and Irish peat bogs, but rarely elsewhere. The Wakehurst bog oak was probably deliberately put into one of the ponds serving local iron-makers, the idea being to store it until it was sawn into planks. Somehow, it was lost; the pond silted up and later became part of the woodland.

Radiocarbon dating from a centre sample showed it to be 1,100 years old, and a ring count, which allowed for some heartwood and sapwood being lost, indicated that the tree had lived for around 230 years before being felled in around 1086, the year the Domesday Book was completed.

THE BURNING QUESTION

Which firewood burns best? This country verse rakes over their various qualities:-

Beechwood fires are bright and clear,
If the logs are kept a year;
Chestnut only good they say,
If for long it's laid away;
Make a fire of *Elder* tree,
Death within your house shall be;
    But *Ash* new or *Ash* old
      Is fit for Queen with crown of gold

Birch and *Fir* logs burn too fast,
Blaze up bright and do not last;
It is by the Irish said,
Hawthorn bakes the sweetest bread;
Elmwood burns like churchyard mould,
E'en the very flames are cold;
    But *Ash* green or *Ash* brown
      Is fit for Queen with golden crown

Poplar gives a bitter smoke,
Fills your eyes and makes you choke;
Apple wood will scent your room,
With an incense-like perfume;
Oaken logs, if dry and old,
Keep away the winter's cold,
    But *Ash* wet or *Ash* dry
      A King shall warm his slippers by.

Anon: Thanks to the "Quote...Unquote"
Newsletter, July 2000

SOFT OR HARD?

Talking timber, softwood comes from conifers and hardwoods are from broad-leaved trees. Softwoods are a range of general purpose timbers used for construction, furniture, cladding, panelling and plywood. Most softwoods deteriorate rapidly outdoors and must be treated or painted, the durable exceptions being those with a high oil content, such as western red cedar and alerce (*Fitzroya cupressoides*), both of which were used to build the SEEBOARD Field Study Centre (see p 88).

Hardwoods are generally mostly used for furniture-making and are valued for their varieties of grain texture, colour and ability to be worked. Many produce outstanding veneers. Some hardwoods, such as sweet chestnut and English oak, can be used as construction timber; others, like lime, are fragile but can be beautifully carved.

To add a little intrigue, yew is classified as a softwood, although it is harder than many so-called hardwoods; and balsa wood, so beloved of model aeroplane makers, is in fact a hardwood.

RING FOR A DATE

Dendrochronology is the science of using tree rings to date structures or events and to discover past environmental conditions. Dates have been determined for past volcanic and glacial activity, avalanches, epidemics of tree disease, forest fires, floods, historical architecture and wooden panels used for oil paintings. A tree ring is a year's growth and the ring is wider when the tree is in strong growth, so ring width gives a good clue as to the environment at that time. Ring-width patterns are unique for particular time periods and in Europe, there is a continuous series of about 7,300 years for buried oak, which is how the Wakehurst bog oak was dated.

Dendrochronology was instrumental in discovering a flaw in the radiocarbon dating method. When the radiocarbon time scale was checked against dated bristlecone pine wood, discrepancies of about 700 years occurred at about 5000 BC.

The history of Wakehurst

High on a ridge, facing the warm south-west, benefiting from a sandy well-drained soil and clean water constantly available from springs - it is little wonder that early man found this part of the High Weald a congenial place to live.

Charcoal remains and ironstone mine pits in the surrounding countryside suggest that Iron Age man lived and worked here, and may well have found the rocky crevices above Bloomer's Valley ideal for winter quarters, once they had been snugly roofed with branches and bracken.

Ancient records tell that the Roman road from *Portus adurni* (Aldrington) to *Anicetis* (Croydon) came by the estate, and aerial photographs also show its route quite clearly running by the South of England Showground.

The name Wakehurst is of Saxon origin:- 'hyrst' meaning wood and 'wake' possibly coming from 'wak', meaning moist or watery. The first written links of Wakehurst with Ardingly came in 1205 when a William de Wakehurst purchased a virgate and a quarter of land in the Parish of Ardingly from Phillip de Crauele

(Crawley). It is reasonable to assume that the Wakehursts built a substantial dwelling and lived there until the line ended in two girls, Margaret and Elizabeth Wakehurst.

Abduction by Culpepers

Placed in the charge of Sir John Culpeper of Bedgebury, the sisters were abducted in 1463 by his brothers Richard and Nicholas who appeared, in the description of the day, "with force and arms riotously against the King's peas arrayed in manner of warre." It is natural that, "the seide Margaret and Elizabeth at the tyme of their takyng away makying grete and pittious lamentacion and wepying", but surprisingly, the distress did not last overlong, since the girls speedily married their abductors and the couples lived together at Wakehurst for nearly 50 years. Margaret, who had no children, died in 1509. Elizabeth seemed to have ensured the continuation of the Culpeper line for some time to come by having no fewer than eighteen children.

The Culpepers were a large and well-respected noble family dating from at least the reign of King John. Today, the best-

Place

known is Nicholas Culpeper (1616-54), the herbalist and author of *The English Physician* and the *Complete Herbal*, but during his lifetime he was merely a distant relative and not highly regarded. Finally, in spite of the potential for family growth given to them by Elizabeth, the line ended in 1740 with the death of the bachelor Sir William Culpeper, a wastrel who had been forced to sell his vast estates to pay off his gambling debts.

BUILDING AND REBUILDING

In 1590 - the date over the door by the Chapel - Edward Culpeper completed the present house, finishing the work started some 20 years earlier by his father, Thomas. The exact format of the Culpeper house cannot be verified, but excavations in 1905 suggested a completely enclosed courtyard entered through an opening in the south wing.

The excavations found a superb Elizabethan dressed stone culvert leading from the courtyard and wings to an outlet by the Slips and a 17th century brick culvert from the kitchen area of the house into the present Mansion Pond.

Building and rebuilding would have been a relatively easy process at Wakehurst Place, since there is sandstone around 60 cm (2 ft) deep in parts of the estate. The house is built from stone quarried either from the Dog Kennel Pits by the Pinetum, or from the pit - now a pond - by the south drive.

In 1848, the east and west wings were drastically shortened because the weight of the heavy Horsham stone roof became too much for the rafters and soft sandstone walls. The existing faces were removed and replaced on the ends of the truncated wings and the demolished stone walls were used to build Newhouse Farm. This is how the house as it stands today came to be.

The history of Wakehurst

A SUCCESSION OF OWNERS

The purchaser of Wakehurst Place from Sir William Culpeper was Dennis Lydell, who became Commissioner of the Navy and a friend and associate of Samuel Pepys. He bought other land around Wakehurst and the estate grew under him and his heirs until in 1748, it covered 3,100 acres (1,255 hectares).

In 1757, it passed to the Clarkes of Blake Hall in Essex, who were relatives of the last of the Rydells, the Rector of Ardingly, and, after the Clarkes, to relatives of theirs, the Peytons, a distinguished military and naval family who had virtually deserted Wakehurst Place as a home by 1821.

For nearly 50 years, the house changed tenants frequently and gradually fell into a rather dilapidated state until 1869, when it was bought by Lady Downshire, the first occupant for many years to bring significant benefit to the estate. In making it a comfortable country seat, she virtually gutted the interior, changed the uses of the principal rooms and even moved the staircase. She also repositioned many of

Place

the garden features and changed the approach to the house to its present layout.

Lady Downshire sold the house, advertised as being 'heated throughout by hot water' in 1890 to Thomas Boord, MP for Greenwich. Sir Thomas William Boord, as he later became, and his wife restored and improved the house considerably, but took little interest in the gardens, which were merely maintained until Gerald Loder, later Lord Wakehurst, bought the property in 1903 and, as a passionate plantsman, started it on the road to the horticultural eminence it has today. (See pp 82-85 for more on building the collections.)

Lord Wakehurst died in 1936 and the estate was later bought by Sir Henry Price, who, in his turn, spent a great deal restoring the stonework and roof of the Mansion before the Second World War interrupted. Wakehurst became the Advanced HQ of the Canadian Corps from January 1942 to October 1943 (see pp 30-31).

Sir Henry and Lady Eve Price continued the Wakehurst horticultural tradition and in their care the estate became widely admired. In 1963, Wakehurst Place, together with a large endowment, was bequeathed to the National Trust. Then, on 1st January 1965, it was leased for the use of the Royal Botanic Gardens, Kew.

Lady Eve Price kept a close personal attachment to her home and in September 1982, she opened the Lady Price Room, furnished with a display of the antiques she and her husband lived with and used while they were in residence together.

Wakehurst Place - building

Gerald Loder grew up on large estates - his father had bought The High Beeches estate at Handcross in 1847 and Whittlebury in Northamptonshire in 1873. He read Law at Trinity College, Cambridge, and was called to the Bar in 1888. He became the MP for Brighton in 1889, holding several Government positions, and was also a successful businessman and keen sportsman, playing golf, cricket and real tennis.
He married Lady Louise, the eldest daughter of the 10th Duke of St. Albans, in 1890.

He bought Wakehurst Place in 1903 and when his business interests became more pressing, he left politics in 1906. He also devoted himself to horticulture and was fortunate to work with the great Head Gardener, Alfred Coates, after whom Coates Wood is named. The story goes that when Alfred Coates went to the House of Commons for an interview, Loder asked him, "Well, Coates, what shall it be; flowers, or trees and shrubs?" and Coates is said to have replied "I reckon trees and shrubs, sir", and on this exchange, Wakehurst's unique collection, built over 32 years, was founded.

the collections

The general passion for plant collecting had continued from Victorian times, and Loder's main interests were conifers, rhododendrons and Southern Hemisphere plants, particularly from New Zealand. Plants arrived almost daily at Wakehurst; from British nurseries and gardens, or from abroad, as seed from plant collecting expeditions sent to subscribers such as Loder; or as crated plants surviving long sea journeys.

Shared enthusiasm and competition between the great gardens of their day led to an almost explosive increase in the number and variety of plants collected by Loder. His notebooks, preserved at Kew, detail purchases he made, while his 1908 plant catalogue ran to 300 pages, and showed that within five years of purchasing the estate, there were some 3,000 species and cultivars at Wakehurst Place.

While the estate was originally shaped by Gerald Loder, the development undertaken by Sir Henry Price, who bought Wakehurst Place after Gerald Loder, then Lord Wakehurst, died, should not be underestimated.

Sir Henry and Lady Eve Price loved the house and gardens and together, they restored the Mansion and developed the gardens with both skill and enthusiasm. They became formidable plant breeders and major exhibitors at Royal Horticultural Society Shows and several award-winning plants, such as *Viburnum* 'Eve Price' and *Pieris* 'Henry Price' were named after them.

In 1963, when Sir Henry Price bequeathed Wakehurst Place to the nation, it had benefited from just over 60 years' worth of enthusiastic nurturing from owners passionate about plants, and backed by outstanding head gardeners.

Two years later, when it was leased from the National Trust as an additional garden for the Royal Botanic Gardens, Kew, the emphasis changed, as Wakehurst Place gradually grew into its new role; no longer a private estate, but a public botanic garden.

Wakehurst Place - from privat*

Wakehurst Place has an outstanding natural landscape, with contoured valleys, lakes and mature plantings, gardened by private owners for centuries. In 1965, work started to convert the estate to a botanic garden accessible to an interested public. Basic work was carried out - constructing the car park and public entrance, building toilet blocks and a network of hard-surfaced paths.

As further work on the gardens and tree collections progressed, Wakehurst was benefiting from Kew's constant collecting activities, but now with conservation firmly to the forefront. Even in those early days, Kew's scientists were among the first to sound warning shots about the loss of important plants and habitats.

By 1983, there were 10,000 plant species and varieties growing at Wakehurst, representing 187 plant families. The reference collections of birch and southern beeches were established and those for hypericums and skimmia were being planned. The Himalayan Glade and the walled gardens near the Mansion were developing well.

Then, in 1987, life changed somewhat with the unwelcome occurrence of the Great Storm. Overnight, on 15th-16th October, and almost unimaginably, some 15,000 trees were lost at Wakehurst Place alone. Gerald Loder had built shelter belts but they were ineffective against the worst storm since 1703. The winds were strongest in the south east, reaching over 100 kph (63 mph) on the south coast where ships were blown ashore. Technically, this was not a true hurricane, where winds can be double those recorded, but it was a 'one in 300 years event' - so said the experts. But another 'severe storm' swept across England just over two years later, on 25th January, 1990.

It took several years just to clear the damage from these two storms but there was a silver lining in that the new plantings were able to group plants in a different manner; following some of the ideas of an eminent Russian botanist, Armen Takhtajan. He champions the idea of classifying the world's vegetation into distinctive areas, each with its own characteristic groupings of plants. This *phytogeographic* grouping helps concentrate

conservation work on areas with the greatest diversity of unique plants (see pp 34-35).

For example, the new plantings in the Pinetum and in Horsebridge Wood group the trees in geographic areas - these are described in greater detail in their respective sections. New techniques for shelter belts were developed (see pp 56-57) as a result of these storms and today, the estate is better protected than at any time in its past.

The knock-on effect of the storms was to destroy a great deal of habitat for the wildlife - bats in particular being evicted from fallen trees, which led to greater competition for the available holes and crevices from other creatures (see pp 70-71).

Today, Wakehurst Place is again not only a place of great beauty, thanks to tireless work since that dreadful dawn in late 1987, but a model of practical conservation. The completion of the Millennium Seed Bank is the realisation of a dream that will bring nothing but good to endangered plants from these islands and the world. The great men who started and developed this estate would be impressed if they could see Wakehurst Place today. But their spirit lives on, so in a way, perhaps they can.

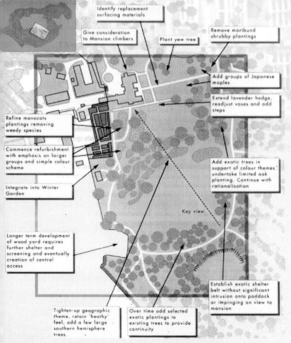

Identify replacement surfacing materials

Give consideration to Mansion climbers

Plant yew tree

Remove moribund shrubby plantings

Add groups of Japanese maples

Extend lavender hedge, readjust vases and add steps

Refine monocots plantings removing weedy species

Commence refurbishment with emphasis on larger groups and simple colour scheme

Integrate into Winter Garden

Add exotic trees in support of colour themes; undertake limited oak planting. Continue with rationalisation

Key view

Longer term development of wood yard requires further shelter and screening and eventually creation of central access

Establish exotic shelter belt without significant intrusion onto paddock or impinging on view to mansion

Tighten-up geographic theme, retain 'heathy' feel, add a few large southern hemisphere trees.

Over time add selected exotic plantings to existing trees to provide continuity

WAKEHURST AND KEW

THE DIFFERENCES THAT MAKE THE DIFFERENCE

At an altitude of 133m (437 ft) above sea level, the rainfall at Wakehurst Place - an average of over 820 mm (32 in) - is half as much again as Kew. Just how much conditions will alter with climate change is a matter for conjecture, but it is reasonably certain that Wakehurst's altitude will consistently make for wetter summers than at Kew. Kew's position in London's own microclimate normally brings warmer winters than at Wakehurst, although in the severe winters of 1947-48 and 1962-63, more tender species survived in the milder climate of the Weald than at Kew. Generally, its winter warmth results in Kew welcoming spring a week or two earlier than at Wakehurst Place, but the Weald's summer moistness gives a longer display of autumn colour at Wakehurst Place. Kew is relatively flat, with a sandy soil that dries out in summer, which allows a great many different plants to be grown. Wakehurst Place has a rich variety of naturally acid soils ranging from clay to sandstone. Its deep clay loam topsoil over a sandstone bed provides an ideal water-retaining - yet well-drained - medium in which its trees and shrubs thrive.

Wakehurst Place - today

As part of the Royal Botanic Gardens, Kew, Wakehurst Place takes a prominent place in a long tradition of botanic gardens. Many, Kew prominent among them, established herbaria containing dried plant specimens used for reference and research and supported botanists on their expeditions to collect, identify and classify the world's plants. This mammoth task has continued over the centuries and today, as the world faces a growing environmental crisis, the work of botanic gardens becomes more deeply involved in conservation and the sustainable use of ecosystems.

PLANT COLLECTIONS

Wakehurst Place has undergone a rapid transition from a private collection to a botanic garden at the forefront of local, national and international conservation. Living collections of plants are a vital part of botanical research and conservation. At Wakehurst Place, the 15,000 different types of plant contain five species that are totally extinct in the wild, and 300 more included in lists of threatened and endangered species.

The living plant collections complement the vast numbers of specimens, both old and recently collected, in Kew's Herbarium and the samples of plant-based artifacts in the Economic Botany Collection. All are invaluable database resources referred to by specialists from all over the world.

CONSERVATION MATTERS

Conservation and sustainable use, nationally and internationally, are the watchwords behind Kew's work today. Kew acts as adviser to the UK government on the Convention on International Trade

and the future

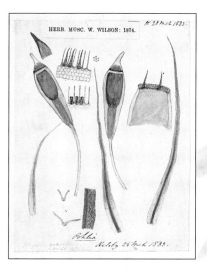

in Endangered Species of Flora and Fauna (CITES) and also on international conservation legislation.

Kew is assisting the UK's conservation agencies with genetic studies on their highest priority species. Conservation genetics is important work, looking at the genetic makeup of populations of endangered plants, to advise on their conservation in the wild, to maximise the retention of genetic diversity and to help design reintroduction programmes.

Kew's work on micropropagation - multiplying plants by reproducing them from seeds, spores and other plant tissue - leading to eventual reintroduction in the wild, is also critically important to biodiversity.

The Wakehurst and Chiddingly Woods SSSI contains various species of interest to plant conservationists, the prime examples being the slender thread moss and Tunbridge filmy fern. Micropropagation is being used to conserve the endangered populations of Tunbridge filmy fern and reintroduction experiments are under way. The slender thread moss is the subject of both genetics studies and micropropagation to conserve and multiply it.

SUSTAINABLE USE

Sustainable use of the world's plant resources is key to their survival for the benefit of future generations. Cultivation of crops, management of wild plants and the harvesting of both should do no damage to either the natural resource base - the plants themselves - or the environment. Kew not only documents traditional and current uses of plants but also explores potential new uses. For example, there is a current study identifying rattans that may be grown as a sustainable crop for use in 'cane' furniture, rather than being taken from diminishing wild sources in rainforests. Also, many of the seeds in the Millennium Seed Bank belong to wild plants that people in the world's drylands rely on for food, fuel or medicine.

Wakehurst Place - today

EDUCATION - PLANTING IDEAS

People visit Wakehurst Place and Kew for a variety of reasons. Casual visitors may come for the beauty, or a breath of fresh air. Garden enthusiasts want to learn more about their particular interests. University students visit to find out more about Kew's research activities, and professionals from all over the world stay for further high level training. It is a rare visitor who leaves the Gardens without being better informed.

Increasing people's understanding of the plant kingdom is vital, so education plays an absolutely key role. So much so, that 'education' at Kew is divided into three: Higher Education and Training; Public Education and Interpretation; and Schools Education, in order to meet the needs of different audiences.

and the future

PUTTING PLANTS ON THE CURRICULUM

If environmental and conservation issues are to be kept alive in this new century, it is vital to inform and influence today's schoolchildren. It is they - tomorrow's consumers, teachers, business people, opinion-formers and politicians - who will be shaping the future of the planet.

More than 60,000 schoolchildren, armed with work sheets and education packs, visit Kew and Wakehurst in booked groups each year.

At Kew, they enjoy the rewards from a tour guided by one of the teaching team or visit the Plants+People Exhibition which regularly astounds visitors of all ages, let alone schoolchildren.

At Wakehurst Place, students of all ages take part in a range of active studies. They may find themselves working around the Mansion, where they take part in plant workshops as well as finding specimens in the garden. Or they may concentrate on habitat studies, visiting the SEEBOARD Field Study Centre set among woods, meadows and wetlands. Here, they combine ecological study with the opportunity to see active conservation management on site. This contrasts well with the study awaiting them when they visit the Millennium Seed Bank.

The Outreach Education Programme sees Kew visiting schools, running anything from week-long specially tailored workshops in a mobile classroom, to a short visit for a talk loaded with specimens and demonstrations and long remembered through the posters and leaflets left behind.

Botany and conservation are very much on today's curriculum. Kew's mission in education is to make the plant kingdom interesting, fun - and important. Caught young, children are conservationists for life.

The work and funding of Kew

KEW'S VITAL WORK

From the 1840s, Kew was engaged in identifying and naming plants and investigating the relationships between them. This research was based on collections of both living and preserved plant materials and the knowledge gained was recorded in illustrations, scientific papers, books and journals. This body of information is a priceless heritage.

The work carried out at Kew from the 1980s onwards, when responsibility was given to a Board of Trustees (1984), has been building up to that being undertaken today, at the start of a new century, when conservation in all its forms has assumed the greatest importance.

Nowhere are Kew's aims more clearly laid down than in the Mission Statement.

Behind the text on these pages runs a simple maxim; "All life depends on plants".

KEW'S MISSION

TO ENABLE BETTER MANAGEMENT OF THE EARTH'S ENVIRONMENT BY INCREASING KNOWLEDGE AND UNDERSTANDING OF THE PLANT AND FUNGAL KINGDOMS - THE BASIS OF LIFE ON EARTH.

This will be achieved by:

- developing our global reference collections and making them more accessible to the greatest possible variety and number of users;

- undertaking world-wide research into systematics, economic and ethnobotany, biological interactions, conservation and horticulture;

- supporting the conservation and sustainable use of plant resources in the UK and overseas;

- informing the wider public about our activities, through the maintenance and development of world-class Gardens that provide a window into our work;

- providing education, advice and information in various forms to our stakeholders, and building the global capacity for studying and conserving plant diversity through collaborative partnerships and by training scientists from developing countries.

Gardens and Wakehurst Place

THE ACT OF CHARITY

The Royal Botanic Gardens, Kew, is a registered charity, set up in April 1984 under the terms of the National Heritage Act, 1983. Responsibility for the Gardens then passed from the Ministry of Agriculture Fisheries and Food (MAFF) to a Board of twelve Trustees.

Kew's functions are broadly defined in an Act of Parliament and are today firmly established in the Mission Statement. Today, the Gardens continue to be funded in part by the Department for Environment, Food and Rural Affairs (DEFRA, which replaced MAFF in 2001). From the late 1980s, the overriding concern at Kew was the securing of additional funds to maintain the Gardens and its research programmes.

Wakehurst Place has been leased from the National Trust since 1965 and the estate is entirely funded and managed by the Royal Botanic Gardens, Kew.

KEW FOUNDATION

In March, 1990, Kew Foundation was set up with the sole aim of raising funds for projects not covered by grant aid and self-generated money. The Foundation has proved an unqualified success, raising in excess of £2 million a year towards Kew projects.

RBG KEW ENTERPRISES LTD

This is the commercial arm of the Gardens, with the sole purpose of generating funds by profitable trading through the Shops at Wakehurst Place and Kew Gardens, from licensing and events such as the Summer Swing music festival at Kew.

Kew Enterprises also manages the hiring out of venues at Kew. Cambridge Cottage is popular for private functions such as weddings, receptions and business meetings; and the Temperate House is also in demand for both private and corporate events.

Profits made from admission fees taken at the gates, catering, events and purchases from the Shops all help support the scientific work undertaken at Kew.

Friends of Kew

KEW'S WORK BENEFITS THE WHOLE WORLD, AND YOU CAN BE PART OF IT.

"Today the Royal Botanic Gardens, Kew, is increasingly involved in the conservation of our environment as thousands of species of plants face extinction. And the simple fact is that without plants, human life on this earth will cease to exist.

Kew's botanists and horticulturists are able to solve global problems by advising on environmental management, conserving endangered species, and searching for alternative crops as sources of food, animal fodder, fuel and medicine.

In supporting the Friends, you will be helping to finance the vital work Kew is doing to help save plant life and the world.

Thank you for your support.

June 1990 saw the launch of Friends of Kew, with membership bringing special privileges and opportunities to those wishing to know more about Kew specifically and horticulture generally.

Members can also accompany Kew botanists through the plant world on a programme of botanical tours; and extend their interest still further with special events and lectures.

Membership income and that generated by fees for various events all contribute much-needed revenue.

Over £3.5 millions have been contributed to Kew through membership, gifts and legacies; revenue which has supported projects like the Millennium Seed Bank, protecting threatened species and numbers of features at both Kew and Wakehurst Place. There's no better way of supporting Kew's mission than to become a Friend.

FRIENDS OF KEW – THE BENEFITS OF BELONGING

For an annual membership fee, Friends of Kew benefit from the following advantages:-

- Unlimited entry to Wakehurst Place, Kew, and fourteen other gardens nationwide.
- KEW magazine four times a year, full of lively articles on horticulture, botany and environmental issues and other interesting subjects.
- Free passes to bring guests into the Gardens.
- Discounts in Wakehurst Place and Kew shops.
- Special events, tours and lectures, plus opportunities to see behind the scenes.

Details on how to join Friends of Kew are in the leaflets available in the Mansion Shop and on the maps handed to visitors on entry.
Or call 020 8332 5922.

For more information

NOTES:

Factual details have been checked by an Editorial Committee at the Royal Botanic Gardens, Kew. Kew Gardens and Wakehurst Place are under constant development, so while the general information in this book is accurate at time of going to press, it will be most up to date from the website and telephone numbers given below.

For ease of reading, the scientific names of plants have generally been omitted from the main body of the text, in favour of common names where they exist.

SOURCES:

The main sources for this souvenir guide have been the leaflets and other communications issued by the Royal Botanic Gardens, Kew; together with the pages and links of Kew's website at www.kew.org

Background information, not directly quoted, has come from a variety of sources.

CONTACTING WAKEHURST PLACE:

Tel: 01444 894066

Fax: 01444 894069

E-mail: wakehurst@kew.org

Web: www.kew.org

FURTHER READING:

There are many leaflets and books available in the Wakehurst Place shop which expand on the information given in this souvenir guide.

LOCATION

Wakehurst Place is around 15 minutes from Junction 10 on the M23, from where it is clearly signposted to just north of Ardingly on the B2028. Haywards Heath station is six miles away by taxi and is served by a regular bus service - for current details call the TraveLine on 0870 608 2 608.

OPENING TIMES AND COSTS

Open from 10 am every day of the year except Christmas Day and New Year's Day. Closing time varies between 4 pm in winter and 7 pm in summer.
For the latest information on times and admission prices, please telephone 01444 894066 (24 hours).

ON-LINE INFORMATION

Visit the website at www.kew.org and click on the information for Wakehurst Place. There's much to be learned about Kew Gardens on the site as well.

CARE FOR THE GARDENS

The estate is here to be explored and the grass is there to be walked on, but please, to protect both the environment and the enjoyment of others, visitors are asked not to handle the plants or climb trees; not to ride bicycles, tricycles, scooters, skates or skateboards; not to play ball games or other sports, nor use radios, or portable music players. No dogs - except guide dogs - are admitted to the estate.

SAFETY & FIRST AID

There are water features in the estate and visitors with small children are asked to be especially watchful for their safety. Some paths are steep and slippery, so please take care especially on damp days. For First Aid or other help, see the staff at the gate, or Mansion Shop, or one of the Rangers. But you will find all Wakehurst staff very willing to help, so if you need a hand, just ask.

WHEELCHAIRS

The paths suitable for wheelchairs are clearly marked on the maps in this book and the admission map.
If in doubt, please consult the map, the map and direction boards throughout the grounds, or ask a member of staff. More information on accessibility is available in advance by telephoning 01444 894000.

PHOTOGRAPHY AND PAINTING

You are welcome to take souvenir photographs or videos, or make drawings and paintings for personal enjoyment. Some favourite viewpoints have been included on the maps in this book, indicated by this symbol. However, any commercial work requires a permit and for an explanation of the cost and conditions, please call 01444 894000.

facts

FOOD AND DRINK

The Stable Restaurant is open throughout the year selling hot and cold drinks, snacks, salads and hot meals which can be enjoyed both inside or outside in a pleasant courtyard. The restaurant normally closes one hour before the gardens.

PICNICS

You are welcome to bring your own picnic to Wakehurst Place and enjoy it at one of the sites provided, or wherever there's a suitable area of flat ground. The only thing asked of you is to be considerate to other visitors and either take litter away with you, or find the nearest rubbish bin and dispose of it properly.

WAKEHURST SHOP

The Mansion Shop is open daily from 10 am, selling a variety of books, cards, stationery, souvenirs, film and postage stamps. Bar-B-Kew charcoal, made from sustainable resources on the Wakehurst estate, is available in spring and summer from the garden shop near the car park, which also sells a wide range of plants and garden products. A range of Wakehurst's estate-grown Christmas trees is available from the first weekend in December.
For more information on the shops, please call 01444 894073.

GUIDED TOURS AND WAKEHURST TRAILS

Guided tours leave the Meeting Point at the Mansion at 11.30 am and 2.30 pm (11.30 am and 2 pm in winter). These may be booked in advance on 01444 894066 for groups of up to 25 people. There are several enjoyable Wakehurst Trails and leaflets describing them and giving a wealth of information on what you can see are available from the Mansion Shop. The Dinosaur's Dinner Trail is a family quiz around the grounds. Many information sheets are also available.

GROUP DISCOUNTS

Groups of ten or more paying visitors may obtain a discount on entry fees by paying in advance. Details and an application form may be obtained by calling 01444 894066. The Stable Restaurant also offers group discount rates, bookable in advance on 01444 894040.

EDUCATION PROGRAMME

Facilities and staff, together with a variety of study packs and teacher training courses, are available to support students on educational visits. More information may be found by visiting the website at www.kew.org or by telephoning 01444 894069.

LODER VALLEY NATURE RESERVE

Entrance to the Reserve is by prior arrangement only. Application forms are available from the entrance and shop, by writing to The Administrator, Wakehurst Place, RH17 6TN, or by telephoning 01444 894066. Ask about special dusk and other visits, but please note that numbers of visitors are strictly limited to protect its standing as a nature reserve.

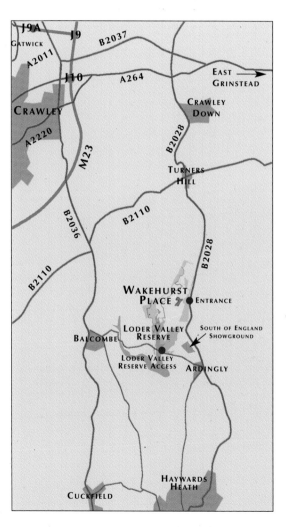

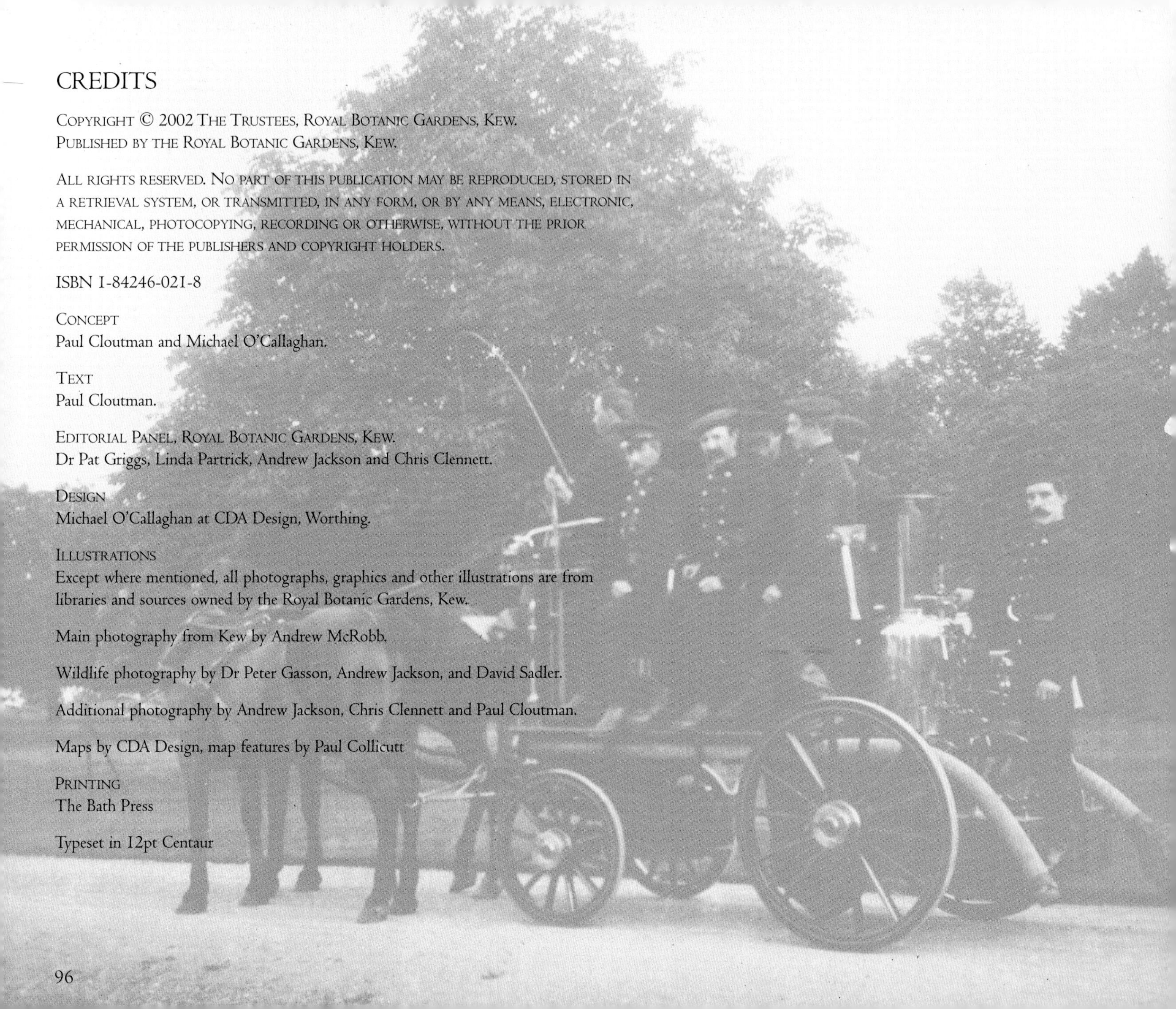

CREDITS

Published by the Royal Botanic Gardens, Kew.

ISBN 1-84246-021-8

Concept
Paul Cloutman and Michael O'Callaghan.

Text
Paul Cloutman.

Editorial Panel, Royal Botanic Gardens, Kew.
Dr Pat Griggs, Linda Partrick, Andrew Jackson and Chris Clennett.

Design
Michael O'Callaghan at CDA Design, Worthing.

Illustrations
Except where mentioned, all photographs, graphics and other illustrations are from libraries and sources owned by the Royal Botanic Gardens, Kew.

Main photography from Kew by Andrew McRobb.

Wildlife photography by Dr Peter Gasson, Andrew Jackson, and David Sadler.

Additional photography by Andrew Jackson, Chris Clennett and Paul Cloutman.

Maps by CDA Design, map features by Paul Collicutt

Printing
The Bath Press

Typeset in 12pt Centaur